W9-CMA-939

a SAVOR THE SOUTH® *cookbook*

Biscuits

SAVOR THE SOUTH® *cookbooks*

Biscuits, by Belinda Ellis (2013)
Bourbon, by Kathleen Purvis (2013)
Tomatoes, by Miriam Rubin (2013)
Peaches, by Kelly Alexander (2013)
Pecans, by Kathleen Purvis (2012)
Buttermilk, by Debbie Moose (2012)

a SAVOR THE SOUTH® *cookbook*

Biscuits

BELINDA ELLIS

The University of North Carolina Press CHAPEL HILL

The paper in this book meets the guidelines for permanence and durability of the Committee on Production Guidelines for Book Longevity of the Council on Library Resources. The University of North Carolina Press has been a member of the Green Press Initiative since 2003.

Library of Congress Cataloging-in-Publication Data
Ellis, Belinda.
Biscuits / by Belinda Ellis.
pages cm. — (A savor the South cookbook)
Includes index.
ISBN 978-1-4696-1066-5 (cloth : alk. paper)
1. Biscuits. 2. Cooking, American — Southern style. I. Title.
TX770.B55E45 2013   641.81′57 — dc23   2013009240

17 16 15 14 13   5 4 3 2 1

To my daughter, Katrina Moore,
who became a foodie despite growing up
with simple meals

Contents

Biscuit Meals 79

EXCUSES TO HAVE BISCUITS FOR DINNER

a SAVOR THE SOUTH® *cookbook*

Biscuits

Introduction

BISCUITS—THE BUTTERY TASTE

OF THE SOUTH

or fifteen years, it was my job to travel around the country and teach people to make biscuits. Armed with my rolling pin and mixing bowls, I had the pleasure of talking to people about their sacred relationship with biscuits. I learned that deep in the soul of a biscuit, there's more than flour, fat, and milk. A hot biscuit embodies a memory of place and family.

In my life, that memory takes me back to the aroma of biscuits, bacon, and sausage coming from the kitchen, my cue to get out of bed on Saturday mornings. Since I slept until breakfast was served, I didn't learn to make biscuits in my youth. As a young bride, I tried to duplicate my mother's breakfast. The biscuits were terrible, and the gravy was a lumpy mess. Finally, as an adult living in a new city, I went back home for a visit and asked my mother to teach me the secrets of making biscuits. There were just a few things I needed to know, and with a little practice, it became easy to make good biscuits.

Little did I know that I would make a career of being "the biscuit lady." I've made biscuits for thousands of people through the years at county fairs, cooking classes, culinary shows, senior expos, and the like. Needless to say, I got plenty of practice.

It doesn't surprise me when people say they just can't make a good biscuit because so many people never had someone to show them how. With that in mind, I've included detailed instructions for making biscuits in the recipes that follow so anyone can do it. My best advice is don't play with the dough—that's the secret to making good biscuits more than anything else.

The old-school bread in the South is trendy across the country now. Go to Tom Douglas's Serious Biscuit in Seattle, Egg in

Brooklyn, or the Biscuit Bus in Nashville and you'll see how cool hot biscuits can be.

Biscuits are humble food to most of us who grew up in the Southeast, made to be served alongside eggs, as dumplings, as a topping for casseroles, with chicken, or for dessert. Sure, there are biscuits in New York City, Seattle, and all places in between, but it's in the South that biscuits *matter*.

Almost every time I taught a biscuit class, someone would come up to me afterward to share a story. They were stories of hands, the mother, grandmother, grandfather whose hands patted out the dough with nothing less than love. Biscuit making is a touch, an art, a simple act of giving. The memories of biscuits live on; they're the stuff of immortality, a remembrance of simple times. The art of making them was once passed down through the family right along with the cast-iron skillets and handmade quilts.

Biscuits hold such a cherished place in southern culture that when a play, book, song, or movie is set in the South, biscuits are sure to have a supporting role. Biscuits symbolize the South.

In any classic southern film or book, biscuits are sure to be on the table. In *The Help* by Kathryn Stockett, biscuits are served up by Minnie as a "cure." In Harper Lee's classic, *To Kill a Mockingbird*, biscuits with syrup are a symbol of equality, as both black and white bystanders at the courthouse eat them for lunch. Pulitzer Prize–winner Eudora Welty often mentions them, such as in *The Optimist's Daughter*, when Laurel is given biscuits from the table to feed to pigeons.

People even sing about biscuits. In the 1930s, blues singer Memphis Minnie sang "I'm Gonna Bake My Biscuits":

I'm gonna bake my biscuits,
Ain't gonna give nobody none.
I'm-a tell you something,
I don't know if I'm wrong or right.
But if you want my bread,
You got to stay all night.

In the 1970s, Kinky Friedman sang the antifeminist song, "Get Your Biscuits in the Oven and Your Buns in the Bed," a sentiment that may have contributed to a decline in the number of women from that generation who cooked.

Quite a few country songs feature biscuits, my personal favorite being Alan Jackson's "Where I Come From":

> Well, I paid the tab and the lady asked me,
> "How'd you like my biscuit?"
> "I'll be honest with you ma'am,
> It ain't like mama fixed it."

On the International Biscuit Festival Facebook page, someone noted that Faith Hill sings a song about "Bis-kits, bis-kits." I searched for the song and couldn't find it, then while listening to her sing "This kiss, this kiss," I realized there had been a little southern misunderstanding of the lyrics! Sometimes biscuit songs are in the hearing rather than the singing.

Few foods have become so enmeshed in southern culture and have made such an impact on the region's history, temperament, and tone of life as biscuits. In the words of author and food historian John Egerton, "There's just nothing else like 'em."

The Rise of Southern Biscuits

What are biscuits? According to Webster's, they're "any of various hard or crisp dry baked products," to which I respond, "Not my biscuits!" But the origin of biscuits predates baking powder, and biscuits used to be very different from the light biscuits we think of now.

What the British call a biscuit, Americans call a cookie. What Americans call a biscuit, the British call a scone. Confused yet?

The word "biscuit" comes from Middle English and early French words meaning twice-cooked bread. Also known as hardtack, the biscuit sustained ship travelers and warriors for centuries.

So how did biscuits as we know them come about? According to John Egerton, the first American biscuits were a cracker-like bread, ¼ to ½ inch thick, usually round, and pricked with a fork, called beaten biscuits. Dining on beaten biscuits was a sign of wealth in the antebellum South for two reasons: flour was expensive to make and transport, and beaten biscuits required the laborious task of bludgeoning the dough with an ax, rolling pin, or other tool for at least thirty minutes until the dough was smooth and slick, a task usually left to slaves or servants. Beaten biscuits weren't the bread of the sharecropper or the farmer—making them required too much effort.

Biscuits as we now think of them—high-rising, light, soft, and tender—came about when people discovered that a mixture of refined ashes from burned wood called pearlash, which left a bitter aftertaste, and later cream of tartar or baking soda with buttermilk created bubbles in baking.

The South adopted biscuits for several reasons. The ingredients were readily available because the wheat that makes the best flour for biscuits grows in southern climates, and lard from easy-to-raise hogs and buttermilk left over from churning butter were easy to come by. Also, biscuits bake much faster than yeast breads, so the oven didn't have to be hot for long, easing the misery of hot summers in the South. In the late 1800s, soft wheat flour was sold in barrels to stores that resold it in 25- or 50-pound cloth sacks, which were reused for clothing and quilts by frugal southern families.

These days, we just eat 'em because they're a part of our family history. John T. Edge in *A Gracious Plenty: Recipes and Recollections from the American South* writes, "The fact remains that when a Southerner reaches for a biscuit or a square of cornbread, he usually reaches for two, ever mindful of that oft-repeated invitation to eat: 'Take two and butter 'em while they're hot.'"

As I traveled and taught the basics of biscuit making, the conversations varied, but there was often a familiar chorus of what biscuits really mean to the southern psyche—they connect us with family. Baking a good biscuit is akin to love. I was often told, "My granny made the best biscuits. She never measured anything, just dumped it all in a bowl. Her biscuits came out perfect every time." Or "My wife made the best biscuits."

But what I heard most often was, "I just can't make a good biscuit." If this is you, you'll love the first recipe in the book, which includes detailed instructions and photographs that almost take you by the hand so you can't fail.

Ingredients

Anytime you're making something with a few simple ingredients—in this case, flour, fat, and liquid—every ingredient counts. The texture and flavor of a biscuit are determined by the choice of ingredient.

FLOUR—THE MAIN INGREDIENT

All flour isn't biscuit flour. It may all look about the same but chemically it isn't, and the type of flour that you select for biscuits makes a huge difference in the resulting texture. This is the first and most important choice in making biscuits.

To understand what type of flour is best for biscuits requires a bit of flour knowledge. Soft winter wheat traditionally grows in southern wheat-growing regions including Kentucky, North Carolina, Ohio, and Missouri. It has less protein than other wheat, which means it has less gluten. Gluten acts like bubble gum—it pulls and stretches. It's this bubble-gum quality that allows yeast to create the air bubbles that are vital for yeast breads. However, gluten is a biscuit maker's worse enemy. Soft biscuits come from soft flour, so the best flour for biscuits is *soft wheat flour*, now often labeled as pastry flour.

All-purpose flour is a blend of soft and hard wheat flours developed with the idea that you can have one type of flour in your pantry that can be used to make anything from yeast breads to cakes. Consequently, it's the most commonly sold flour. In my opinion, flour that's blended is less than ideal for any type of baking. The protein content is too low for yeast breads and too high for biscuits.

White Lily is considered by many to be the best flour for biscuits. Made from 100 percent soft red winter wheat flour (even though it's labeled as all-purpose flour), it was once milled in Knoxville, Tennessee, using a long milling process, an unusual method for soft wheat flour. In days gone by, only half of the flour—the finest half—went into the White Lily bag. "At the turn of the century, the question was, how pure and white can you get it?," one of the former mill operators, Fran Churchill, told the *New York Times* in 2008.

Famed chefs around the country raved about White Lily. Specialty stores such as Williams-Sonoma and the famed Balducci's in New York City offered the flour to their customers.

For more than 100 years, the mill in Knoxville, with its basketball-court-shiny hardwood floors, produced White Lily flour using wooden sifters that hula-hooped continuously inside its five-foot-thick brick walls that held all the magic in. After the J. M. Smucker Company bought the brand in 2007, it closed the Knoxville mill. Reactions to the changes were documented in the *New York Times*, *Atlanta Journal Constitution*, *Knoxville News Sentinel*, and other newspapers throughout the South. People, myself included, rushed to find bags of White Lily flour that were still milled in Knoxville, putting them in their freezers to hang onto each precious grain for as long as possible.

As with any change, opinions vary, and there has been much written about the differences. But you have to salute the J. M. Smucker Company for realizing the brand's worth to southerners. The flour it makes may not be the same flour that White Lily milled 100 years ago, but it still makes a darn good biscuit.

Since I worked for White Lily for many years and then for the J. M. Smucker Company, the maker of Pillsbury, Martha White, Red Band, and Robin Hood as well as White Lily, you might think I'm biased, but I've also been a consultant for other brands of flour. I'm only biased about one thing: FOR BISCUIT MAKING, USE 100 PERCENT SOFT WHEAT FLOUR, NO MATTER WHAT THE BRAND. I used various brands of soft wheat flour or locally milled pastry flour for the recipes in this book, so any soft wheat flour will work with these recipes.

With that being said, there are a few exceptions. If I wanted a layered, flaky biscuit, I used all-purpose flour. This type of biscuit isn't the traditional southern-style biscuit, but it's delicious and worth including. Also, I used all-purpose flour in Angel Biscuits (page 28) because they contain yeast and all-purpose flour makes yeast rise better.

Self-rising flour was really the first biscuit mix because it contains the amounts of baking powder and salt used in biscuits. Some self-rising flours are 100 percent soft wheat, but many are all-purpose blends. However, most use a higher amount of low-protein wheat to make them suitable for biscuit making. If you're using soft wheat flour and want to make it self-rising flour, for every cup of flour, add 1½ teaspoons baking powder and ½ teaspoon salt.

Self-rising flour has a shorter shelf life than soft wheat or all-purpose flour because the baking powder loses its strength over time. If you don't bake often, it's a good idea to purchase flour without the leavening added.

Flour can be kept at room temperature for about a year as long as it's sealed in an airtight container. If you have the freezer space, you can keep it in the freezer forever in an airtight container. Refrigeration in a well-sealed container also increases flour's shelf life.

Finally, it doesn't seem to make much of a difference for biscuits whether flour is bleached or unbleached. I've achieved excellent results with both.

LEAVENING

Baking powder makes biscuits rise, but so does buttermilk when combined with baking soda. Some people like using aluminum-free baking powder such as Rumford because of health concerns or because they prefer the flavor.

FAT

Flakiness and flavor are dependent on the choice of fat, and, of course, there are health considerations as well. I'll let nutritionists guide you on the healthiest choice and limit my discussion to the texture and flavor imparted by each type of fat. Also, fats should always be very cold when making biscuits.

Lard. Rendered lard is available directly from hog producers. The highest grade, leaf lard, is natural and doesn't have much pork flavor, so it's ideal for baking. It has to be either refrigerated or frozen, or it will spoil. Avoid lower-grade supermarket lard, which is usually hydrogenated and bleached and has additives to keep it shelf-stable.

Shortening. Any fat that solidifies at room temperature is called shortening. Almost synonymous with shortening, Crisco (an acronym for crystallized cottonseed oil) was first developed in 1911 by Proctor and Gamble for making soap. Once it's use in baking was discovered, it was widely advertised as cheaper than lard and easier to store because it can be kept at room temperature. The J. M. Smucker Company has owned Crisco since 2002 and has created a new transfat-free shortening. Some claim that biscuits made with the new Crisco aren't as flaky. I've found that freezing it before using it is helpful since the new Crisco is softer at room temperature. I now use an organic nonhydrogenated vegetable shortening and freeze it with good results, or better yet, I use butter.

Butter. Unsalted butter makes a biscuit crisper than shortening or lard and imparts a heavenly flavor. I most often make biscuits using either butter or a mixture of shortening and butter.

BUTTERMILK

According to Debbie Moose in *Buttermilk: A Savor the South Cookbook*, before refrigeration, in hot climates the thin low-fat liquid left over from churning butter was left at room temperature to ferment, creating a tart-flavored acidic milk called buttermilk. The higher acidity meant that it could be stored longer than fresh milk, and southerners often used it for making biscuits.

These days, the process of making the buttermilk that you find in the grocery store is similar to the process of making yogurt in that it's inoculated with bacteria to promote fermentation rather than being a by-product of butter making. It's found in both whole and nonfat varieties, sometimes with butter flakes added. Small local dairies often produce excellent thick buttermilk with good flavor.

I recommend using only whole buttermilk for baking. Give it a quick shake before you use it since it tends to separate. It's important to note that buttermilk varies in thickness so you'll need to adjust the amount of liquid you use in a recipe to achieve the desired dough consistency.

If you don't have buttermilk, in a pinch you can make acidified milk by adding 1 tablespoon lemon juice or white vinegar to 1 cup milk and letting it stand for 10 minutes.

Tools and Equipment

Biscuits are simple food, and biscuit makers usually believe in making do with what they have—a bowl and your hands work just fine for mixing the dough, and any baking pan will do. That being said, through the years I've used many tools and gadgets. These are my favorites.

Bowl: Use a large bowl so that the flour is only about 3 or 4 inches deep. The process of cutting in the fat is easier if you have a wider area to work in so you don't have to work so deep in the bowl. Many great biscuit bakers have a favorite bowl they use every time they make biscuits.

Pastry blender: Your fingertips work fine to break up the fat, but they're warm. This is a problem when you want a flaky biscuit because it's the melting of the fat during baking that creates a flaky biscuit. A cold metal tool is best for the job. The best pastry blenders have solid metal sides with cutting blades at the bottom.

Biscuit cutter: Many people use a drinking glass to cut biscuits. A glass does cut biscuits, but the rim of a glass is rounded rather than sharp so it pinches the edges of the dough and the biscuits end up not rising as much on the sides. Good biscuit cutters have sharp edges that make a clean cut. You can use any size biscuit cutter you want, from tiny to huge. Also, who said biscuits have to be round? Why not make square biscuits?

Dough scraper: When used around the edge of a bowl to toss the flour into the wet ingredients, a bowl scraper, a plastic tool with a curved edge, is a simple way to avoid overstirring the dough. Most restaurants that make biscuits use a dough scraper, but dough scrapers are rarely seen in home kitchens. They usually cost only about $2.00, and you can find them in baking catalogs and some kitchen stores.

Bench knife: Another useful tool seldom seen in a home kitchen is a bench knife, a metal square with a handle. When dough sticks to a surface, you can use a bench knife to loosen it. You can also use a bench knife to clean the flour off your counter.

Rolling surface: It's certainly not a must, but it's nice to have a surface you can use to roll out your dough on that can be easily moved to the trashcan and then the sink for cleaning. There are silicone surfaces designed for rolling, or you can use a cutting board, wax paper, or parchment paper. However, a kitchen counter works just fine, especially if you have a bench knife or dough scraper to scrape off the flour.

Baking pans: I usually use a cake pan for baking biscuits because the high sides make the biscuits rise higher. Baking sheets with sides are my second choice. A dark pan makes the bottoms brown more. If you like crisp biscuits, use a dark pan, even cast-iron, but watch the biscuits carefully to make sure the bottoms don't burn.

Classic Biscuits, Any Way You Like

The ideal biscuit is usually the one you grew up eating. I was lucky enough to be raised around more than one type of biscuit, so I love them all.

My mom's biscuits were made with shortening and rolled out, so they were tall and light. My grandmother's biscuits were made with lard and were shaped by hand to be thin and too tender for this world. Later, my mom decided that it was okay to serve biscuits that came from a can, and I learned to pull the flakes apart and eat each layer one by one. By the time she discovered frozen biscuits, I had learned to make my own, so I never adapted to that too-much-baking-powder aftertaste of commercially made frozen biscuits.

"You just aren't doing it right" was an oft-repeated comment by students in my biscuit classes, who would then explain the "right" way. Every touch and turn of the dough creates a different texture, every change in ingredient a different flavor. The recipe that begins this section is my take on the classic biscuit recipe, but there are more ways to make biscuits than I could ever include in this book. These biscuits are soft and light, the pretty high-rising biscuits you find in restaurants that are known for their biscuits. It's the recipe that I found through the years of teaching biscuit making that people most often wanted to learn.

Some of the following recipes are heirloom recipes, a link to our southern histories, recipes passed down from generations past. They're recipes graciously shared for the rest of us to enjoy. Others are designed for simplicity. All of them are worthy of praise.

Experiment, get your hands dirty, bake them all, and find your favorites. They're all delicious.

Southern Biscuits Step-by-Step

It will take more time to read this recipe than it will take to actually make the biscuits. The simple steps explain the basic technique of biscuit making, and the accompanying photographs show you what the key steps look like. The recipe isn't as difficult as it looks—it simply gives all the details you need to know to bake a good biscuit.

This isn't the only way to make great biscuits, but it's a good way to get started, to get the feel of the dough, to learn how moist you should make the dough and how much to handle it—the keys to making a perfect biscuit.

MAKES 12 BISCUITS

---

2 cups soft wheat self-rising flour
5 tablespoons vegetable shortening, unsalted butter, or lard,
   cut into ½-inch chunks and chilled for 15 minutes
¾ cup whole buttermilk, plus more if needed
All-purpose flour for dusting
Melted butter for brushing the tops

Preheat the oven to 500°. If you have a convection oven, preheat it to 425°. If you're using a silicone or parchment paper liner, don't bake at a temperature higher than 425°. Turn the oven on before you start to make the biscuits because preheating the oven will take longer than making the biscuits and you don't want to let the dough sit while you wait for the oven to preheat because the leavening will start to react and lose its effectiveness in baking.

Spoon the flour lightly into a nesting-type measuring cup. (If you use the measuring cup to scoop the flour, you'll get too much flour.) Level the flour using a flat utensil such as a pastry

knife or bench knife. (See photo ❶.)

Pour the flour into a large shallow bowl to make the process of cutting in the fat easier. Sprinkle the cold chunks of shortening, butter, or lard over the flour. Use a pastry blender or your fingertips to break up the chunks, but don't overwork the dough. If using your hands, work fast so you don't melt the fat.

The fat will create the flakes in the biscuits as it melts between the baked layers of dough, so you want the chunks to be pebbly. Shake the bowl, which will make the larger pieces rise to the top, and continue working in the fat until all the chunks are pea-sized. (See photo ❷.)

Up to this point, you really can't go wrong, but be sure to follow the instructions for adding the liquid and shaping the dough very carefully to avoid making a hard biscuit. Every time you stir, fold, pat, or touch the dough in any way, you're making the biscuits less tender.

Make a well in the center of the bowl and add the buttermilk (photo ❸). Toss the flour over the liquid with a spatula or dough scraper and continue tossing the mixture together. Don't stir.

At this point, you'll have to determine whether to add more liquid. A recipe can't tell you exactly how much liquid to add because the fat content of the milk, the amount of protein in the flour, and even the weather can affect the moistness of the dough. Biscuit dough has the right amount of liquid when it pulls away from the sides of the bowl, is wet but not runny and sticky, and looks messy, a bit like wet sand for a sandcastle.

(See photo .) It shouldn't be smooth like yeast dough or cookie dough.

If the dough is too wet, toss in a dusting of flour and keep on tossing in more flour until it looks right. If the dough is too dry, add more liquid and toss with the flour until it's just wet.

Once the liquid has been incorporated into the dough, lightly dust a rolling surface with all-purpose flour. I use all-purpose flour because the leavening in self-rising flour gives biscuits a bad flavor. The type of surface doesn't really matter as long as it's dry and smooth—a countertop is fine—but the amount of flour does. Use the smallest amount of flour possible, then place the dough on the flour.

Now make a pile of flour near the dough—bakers call this bench flour. Dust your hands with some of the flour to keep the dough from sticking to your hands.

To knead the dough, cuddle it with your floured hands (photo ), then pat the top, pressing lightly to flatten it about ¼ inch thick. Pick up the right side of the dough and fold it a third of the way toward the center. Pick up the left side and fold it over the right side like a letter (photo ⑥). Fold the back side of the dough a third of the way toward the front (photo ⑦) and then fold again.

Pick up the dough, using a bench knife if it sticks to the surface. Dust the surface underneath the dough lightly with more flour. Place the dough down and pat it again (photo ❽), repeating the folding steps.

Kneading biscuit dough isn't the same as kneading bread dough. A bit of kneading makes biscuits flaky, but the less you handle the dough, the lighter the biscuit.

If you want a smooth top, use a floured rolling pin to roll the dough ½ to 1 inch thick, depending on how tall you want the biscuits to be. Use a light touch to roll the dough because if you press too hard, you'll make the dough sticky. If you prefer rougher tops, gently press the dough with your hands to the desired thickness (photo ❾).

To cut the biscuits, flour a 2-inch biscuit cutter. Press the cutter into the dough without twisting it (photo ❿), then pick up the biscuit (photo ⓫). If it sticks, loosen it with a bench knife or metal spatula. Cut the biscuits as closely together as possible. When all the dough has been cut, pick up the scraps of dough (photo ⓬) and, with as little handling as possible, press them back together and cut out the remaining biscuits.

Place the biscuits on a nonstick cake pan or baking sheet. If you want soft sides, place the biscuits so they touch; if you want crisp sides, place them about ½ inch apart.

Bake the biscuits in the center of the oven for about 8 minutes for a 2-inch cutter, 12 minutes for a 3-inch cutter, and 16 minutes for a 4-inch cutter. If you're using soft wheat flour, the biscuits are done when the tops are very light brown. If you're using flour with more protein, the biscuits are done when the tops are dark golden brown. The best way to check for doneness is to look at the bottom of a biscuit to see if it's brown and break one open to determine if the inside is no longer doughy.

Brush the tops with melted butter as soon as the biscuits come out of the oven and remove them from the pan. The butter will brown a bit, making the top more golden brown. Serve immediately.

Nannie's Pinch Biscuits

The real way to make the iconic southern biscuit is this way. If you're looking for your grandmother's recipe, this just might be it. Women from generations past shaped biscuits by hand as they worked the dough to light perfection. It was an art.

I had the good fortune to grow up with a grandmother, Nannie, who made biscuits this way. She showed me her method, but I never really got it. It was while watching other great biscuit makers like her, usually with old hands that quickly shaped the dough, that I finally saw the touch needed to make a great biscuit.

These biscuit artists learned through lots of practice. They weren't afraid to try, fail, and try again, a good lesson to learn!

These biscuits are amazingly tender, but don't expect them to rise up tall. They're flat and crisp, with a soft texture inside.

Nannie always used lard in her biscuits, but shortening or butter is also fine. If you use lard, make sure it's the highest quality.

MAKES 16 BISCUITS

3½ cups soft wheat self-rising flour
¾ cup whole buttermilk
¼ cup lard
Melted butter for brushing the tops

Preheat the oven to 500°. (My grandmother put her hand carefully into the oven to see if it felt right, a habit left over from having a woodstove growing up.) Use a nonstick cake pan or baking sheet.

Sift the flour into a large flat bowl. (Nannie had a canister of flour and a sifter built into a cabinet, often known by its brand name, Hoosier Cabinet. Many people had carved wooden bowls, but my grandmother never had one. She had a favorite red mixing bowl.)

Make a large well in the center, about enough to hold 1½ cups. Pour in about half of the buttermilk. Place the lard in the buttermilk. (Many older bakers use their hands to scoop out the fat and say to use about the size of a walnut, but they mean a walnut off the tree in its outer shell.)

With your fingertips in the buttermilk, break up the lard into chunks, then use a pinching and pressing motion to flatten them. Do this quickly or the lard will begin to melt. Continue until the fat and buttermilk are well mixed. It's okay if some flour starts to fall into the mixture. (Your hand gets messy, so as a kid this step looked like fun. As she worked, Nannie often told me stories of using flour sacks to make clothing when she was a child. She said the clothes were "scratchy" and a sign of being poor.)

Toss some of the flour from the sides of the well into the buttermilk mixture with your hands. You'll think it's not working, but continue adding flour, keeping the ball of dough in the center and the dry flour to the outside of the bowl. Add the remaining buttermilk gradually as you toss in the flour.

Keep working in the flour by rolling the dough around gently only until the dough feels right—you won't use all of the flour in the bowl. The dough should feel like a marshmallow—soft but not too soft. This part is by feel, so it takes practice.

(When the dough was right, Nannie would scoop out a bit of dry flour from the side of the bowl with her hand and go to the trashcan. Over the trashcan, she would rub her hands together with the flour to "wash" them. I often use this method of hand cleaning when baking.)

Pinch off pieces of dough, making them about the size of a golf ball so they'll all take the same amount of time to bake. As soon as you pinch a piece of dough, dip it into the flour at the edge of the bowl.

Place the ball of dough in the palm of your nondominant hand, then cup your dominant hand over it and rotate it to form a biscuit. Handle the dough only enough to shape it, then use your pinkie and thumb to "cuddle" it.

Place the biscuits on the cake pan or baking sheet, close together for taller biscuits or farther apart for flatter, crisper biscuits. Then give them a little pat with your floured hand so they're about ½ inch thick. (I'm not sure whether this is important, except that when Nannie did it, it seemed like the final touch, like a love pat.) Some people put a thumb in the center so the top doesn't rise more in the center than along the sides.

Bake for 8–12 minutes, depending on the size, until golden brown. Brush the tops with melted butter and serve to your family to create a memory.

Sharon Benton's
Perfect-for-Country-Ham Biscuits

You'll never taste country ham better than Benton's Smoky Mountain Country Ham in Madisonville, Tennessee. The cinderblock building with the old sign on US 411 is as unassuming as its owner, Allan Benton. "It's all about quality, and I want to make ham and bacon the best I can for as long as I can," Allan told me on the phone right before the Christmas holiday, when he was working long hours to supply everyone from local folks who park all around the place to get in the door to fine restaurants around the country. That's the secret behind his ham—personal attention to quality and hard work with a dose of humility and gratefulness. Allan and his hams are amazing.

A lot has been written about this man who makes perfect hams. But for the perfect biscuits to go with his ham, I knew to call his wife Sharon. Allan says Sharon made light biscuits "before she married an ol' hillbilly like me." I spoke to Sharon on a Saturday just before Christmas while Allan was working long hours at the ham house and she was home with her daughters and granddaughters making cinnamon rolls and candy, which made me want to drop by for a visit. Equally humble, kind, friendly, and hardworking, Sharon is an administrator for the school system in rural Monroe County.

Sharon grew up in 4-H, making fluffy biscuits and even giving demonstrations, but when she married Allan, she learned to make biscuits a new way from his mother. Her mother-in-law's biscuits are about ¼ inch tall and "hard as a rock," she said. "His mother says babies can cut their teeth on them."

Sharon explained, "You don't want too much biscuit when you're eating them with country ham." But she learned to make biscuits that are lighter than Allan's mother's biscuits using the same simple method, which doesn't include shortening. She laughed, "I guess it's just lazy, but heck, if you don't have to cut that shortening in, you can just add the buttermilk and go." The texture is perfect for country ham—it doesn't fall apart when you eat it. She warned that not just any flour or any buttermilk will work.

She uses locally produced Cruze Dairy buttermilk and a North Carolina milled flour called Our Best, since the flour mill sixteen miles from her house closed. She doesn't measure, so I approximated the recipe.

She makes them small, about two inches wide, and serves them with cream gravy made from rendered fat from country ham or sausage. "I finally got Allan to bring me extra pieces of ham fat to render for gravy," she said. Her recipe is about the same as Grandma's Gravy (page 124), except she uses either ham fat or sausage fat, depending on what she's making at the time.

Most of us can't get the buttermilk she uses, but it's very important to use whole, rich, thick buttermilk or the resulting biscuit will be tough. You'll have to make the biscuits yourself, but you can get the country ham, most days simply by calling Allan to place an order.

MAKES ABOUT 12 BISCUITS

2 cups soft wheat self-rising flour
1 cup whole buttermilk or 1–2 tablespoons heavy cream plus
    enough whole buttermilk to equal 1 cup
All-purpose flour for dusting
Melted margarine for brushing the tops

Preheat the oven to 350°. Use a nonstick cake pan or baking sheet.

Measure the flour into a mixing bowl.

Make a well in the center and pour in the buttermilk. Starting at the sides of the bowl, use a spatula or wooden spoon to toss the flour over the buttermilk. Continue to work in the flour from the sides of the bowl, just until the dough comes together.

If the dough starts to pull away from the sides of the bowl and sticks to your fingers, you have the right amount of buttermilk. If there are dry spots and the dough isn't sticky when you touch it, add more buttermilk.

Dust a surface with all-purpose flour and turn the dough out onto the surface. Flour your hands, then cuddle the dough by pressing your hands around the outer edges. Pat and press the top of the dough with your floured hands. Fold the dough in half, pat it, and fold it again. Repeat this two or three times until the outside of the dough feels less sticky and becomes smooth.

Press the dough gently to the desired thickness: ½ inch for traditional biscuits or up to 1 inch for very tall biscuits.

Cut the biscuits using a 2-inch biscuit cutter without twisting the cutter. Place the biscuits in the cake pan or baking sheet so they touch if you like soft sides or about ½ inch apart for crisper sides.

Combine the leftover pieces of dough and cuddle them with your hands, handling the dough as little as possible. Cut out more biscuits. Form the remaining scraps into a snake and place it around the biscuits. This will make the biscuits rise more evenly. (And the snake makes a crispy extra for the cook.)

Brush the tops with melted margarine.

Bake the biscuits in the center of the oven until they're light golden brown, 10–12 minutes. Stuff with country ham.

Lazy Biscuits

Dropping biscuits onto a baking sheet rather than rolling out the dough on a countertop is nice and quick. Drop biscuits have the added bonus of having a crispy top. I often use this recipe in hands-on classes for beginning bakers because it always yields perfect results. Dropping the biscuits eliminates the common mistake of playing with the dough too much.

After we made these biscuits in one class, a woman announced in a loud voice, "Those are lazy biscuits." She said she still rolls out her biscuits every day, even at the age of eighty-nine. Then she admitted that, well occasionally, when her boys were young . . .

I couldn't argue—these are lazy. My Lazy Biscuits have provided a quick breakfast on many mornings. We love the supercrisp tops and tender insides.

MAKES 8 BISCUITS

---

2 cups soft wheat self-rising flour
6 tablespoons vegetable shortening, unsalted butter, or lard,
    cut into 1/2-inch chunks and chilled for 15 minutes
3/4 cup whole buttermilk, plus more if needed
Melted butter for brushing the tops

Preheat the oven to 500°. Use a nonstick cake pan or baking sheet.

Measure the flour into a large mixing bowl. Add the cold chunks of shortening, butter, or lard and toss them in the flour to coat. Using a pastry blender or your fingertips, break up the chunks until they're about the size of peas.

Make a well in the center and pour in the buttermilk. Starting at the sides of the bowl, use a spatula or wooden spoon to toss the flour over the buttermilk. Continue to work in the flour from the sides of the bowl, just until the dough comes together.

If the dough starts to pull away from the sides of the bowl and sticks to your fingers, you have the right amount of buttermilk. If there are dry spots and the dough isn't sticky when you touch it, add more buttermilk.

Using an ice cream scoop or heaping tablespoon, drop the biscuits onto the cake pan or baking sheet. Since these biscuits are crisp, drop each scoop about a ½ inch apart.

Bake the biscuits in the center of the oven until they're light golden brown, 8–10 minutes. Brush the tops with melted butter.

I-Can't-Believe-Biscuits-Can-Be-This-Easy Cream Biscuits

It seems too good to be true that you can simply mix cream and flour to make a biscuit. When I found this recipe in a dusty old file cabinet in a back storage room at White Lily Flour Company about twenty years ago, I didn't think it would work. After trying the recipe, though, I wondered why everyone doesn't use it to make biscuits. It bakes up tender and moist with very little effort because you don't have to cut in the shortening.

When my daughter, Katrina Moore, moved to Seattle, her roommates enjoyed her biscuits, which she made as an occasional treat. Finally, she tired of their begging for biscuits and taught them this simple recipe. One Christmas morning, she got a call from a former roommate, John Huddleston, who asked, "How much cream is it you add?" Getting that type of phone call lets you know that you've "arrived" as a true biscuit maker. I was thrilled to see the tradition being passed along.

Cream biscuits don't brown much, so don't overbake them. They're tender but not flaky. This won't stop anyone from enjoying every bite.

MAKES ABOUT 12 BISCUITS

2 cups soft wheat self-rising flour

1–3 teaspoons sugar (optional)

1 cup heavy whipping cream, plus more for brushing the tops

All-purpose flour for dusting

Melted butter for brushing the tops

Preheat the oven to 450°. Use a nonstick cake pan or baking sheet.

Measure the flour into a large mixing bowl and whisk in the sugar, if desired.

Make a well in the center and pour in the cream. Starting at the sides of the bowl, use a spatula or wooden spoon to toss the flour over the cream. Continue to work in the flour from the sides of the bowl, just until the dough comes together.

If the dough starts to pull away from the sides of the bowl and sticks to your fingers, you have the right amount of cream. If there are dry spots and the dough isn't sticky when you touch it, add more cream.

Dust a surface with all-purpose flour and turn the dough out onto the surface. Flour your hands, then cuddle the dough by pressing your hands around the outer edges. Pat and press the top of the dough with your floured hands. Fold the dough in half, pat it, and fold it again. Repeat this two or three times until the outside of the dough feels less sticky and becomes smooth.

Use a rolling pin or pat the dough to flatten it to the desired thickness: ½ inch for traditional biscuits or up to 1 inch for very tall biscuits.

Cut the biscuits using a 2-inch biscuit cutter without twisting the cutter. Place the biscuits in the cake pan or baking sheet so they touch if you like soft sides or about ½ inch apart for crisper sides.

Combine the leftover pieces of dough and cuddle them with your hands, handling the dough as little as possible. Cut more biscuits. Form the remaining scraps into a snake and place it around the biscuits. This will make the biscuits rise more evenly. (And the snake makes a crispy extra for the cook.)

Brush the tops with a bit of cream.

Bake the biscuits in the center of the oven until they're light golden brown, 10–12 minutes. Brush the tops with melted butter.

Angel Biscuits

I've always loved these biscuits, folded in the center and brushed heavily with butter. A woman who worked in the Carson-Newman College cafeteria, whose name I've long ago forgotten, was making them one day and I stopped to tell her that her rolls were awesome. "Why these are nothin' but just simple angel biscuits," she told me. I told her that they were more like devil biscuits because I had gained about ten pounds since coming to college, although I can't completely blame the biscuits.

Not many people will tell you that they looked for a recipe for college-cafeteria food, but these are exceptional. I think you'll love them too. Just don't blame me if you can't stop eating them. The longer you let the dough sit in the refrigerator, the better the flavor. They're very much like yeast rolls, a light and flaky cross between biscuits and rolls.

The origin of the recipe is claimed by two old Tennessee flour companies. Emory Thompson told me that he invented the recipe while working for White Lily because the yeast and baking powder made the biscuits failure proof. Then I met Linda Carman, who told me that someone at Martha White claimed to be the inventor. As with many recipes, there are many claims and many names. But when you get a hankering for a roll that's easy to make, you won't care who invented these.

MAKES ABOUT 2 DOZEN BISCUITS

- 1 package active dry yeast
- 2 tablespoons warm water (105°–115°)
- 2 cups warm buttermilk (105°–115°)
- 5 cups soft wheat self-rising flour
- ¼ cup sugar
- 1 stick unsalted butter, cut into ½-inch chunks and chilled for 15 minutes
- ½ cup vegetable shortening, cut into ½-inch chunks and chilled for 15 minutes

All-purpose flour for dusting
Melted butter for brushing the middles and tops

Use a nonstick cake pan or baking sheet.

Sprinkle the yeast over the warm water and let it stand for 10 minutes. Add the buttermilk and stir.

Measure the flour into a large mixing bowl and whisk in the sugar. Add the cold chunks of butter and shortening and toss them in the flour to coat. Using a pastry blender or your fingertips, break up the chunks until they're about the size of peas.

Make a well in the center and pour in the buttermilk mixture. Starting at the sides of the bowl, use a spatula or wooden spoon to toss the flour over the buttermilk. Continue to work in the flour from the sides of the bowl, just until the dough comes together.

Refrigerate the dough overnight or up to 3 days.

Preheat the oven to 425°.

Dust a surface with all-purpose flour and turn the dough out onto the surface. Flour your hands, then cuddle the dough by pressing your hands around the outer edges. Pat and press the top of the dough with your floured hands. Fold the dough in half, pat it, and fold it again. Repeat this two or three times until the outside of the dough feels less sticky and becomes smooth.

Use a rolling pin or pat the dough to flatten it ¼ inch thick, brush it with melted butter, and fold it in half.

Cut the biscuits using a 3-inch biscuit cutter without twisting the cutter. Brush each biscuit with butter and fold in half into a half-moon shape. Place the biscuits close together in the cake pan or baking sheet. Cover with a lint-free cloth in a warm place and let rise until doubled in size, about 1 hour. (The dough will leave an indention when lightly pressed with your finger.)

Bake the biscuits in the center of the oven until they're light golden brown, 15 minutes. Brush the tops with melted butter.

Cat Head Biscuits

"Come and get a fresh-baked cat head" has been blasted from a microphone for decades at the Mississippi State Fair. If you haven't heard the term before, you might find this announcement alarming. But the nearly 100,000 people who line up each year for the free handmade biscuits know that cat heads are big biscuits worth standing in line for. The State Agriculture Department workers who man the booth poke holes in the sides of the biscuits with a device designed just for the job and fill them to order with syrup.

When I attended the fair each year, I heard stories from people whose parents took them to the booth for biscuits and who now bring their own children—another tradition built around biscuits.

The name comes from being as large as a cat's head, though most biscuits now are nearly that size, including fast-food biscuits.

They're shaped by hand, so they're never pretty, picture-perfect biscuits. But they're light and tender, and big, very big.

MAKES 12 LARGE BISCUITS

---

4 cups soft wheat self-rising flour
$\frac{1}{2}$ cup vegetable shortening, cut into $\frac{1}{2}$-inch chunks and
 chilled for 15 minutes
$1\frac{1}{2}$ cups whole buttermilk, plus more if needed
Melted butter for brushing the tops

Preheat the oven to 500°. Use 2 nonstick cake pans or a baking sheet.

Measure the flour into a large mixing bowl. Add the cold chunks of shortening and toss them in the flour to coat. Using a pastry blender or your fingertips, break up the chunks until they're about the size of peas.

Make a well in the center and pour in the buttermilk. Starting at the sides of the bowl, use a spatula or wooden spoon to toss the flour over the buttermilk. Continue to work in the flour from the sides of the bowl, just until the dough comes together.

If the dough starts to pull away from the sides of the bowl and sticks to your fingers, you have the right amount of buttermilk. If there are dry spots and the dough isn't sticky when you touch it, add more buttermilk.

Flour your hands and pinch off pieces of dough or use a ¼-cup scoop. Place the biscuits in the cake pans or baking sheet and pat them with a floured hand.

Bake the biscuits in the center of the oven until they're light golden brown, 8–12 minutes. Brush the tops with melted butter.

Petite Tea Biscuits

Growing up in the South, you never attended a wedding or shower that didn't serve small biscuits filled with ham. If you go to a tearoom, you'll find a similar ham biscuit on the menu. Use country ham slices for the traditional finishing touch. The sugar in this biscuit tastes good with the ham, but if the ham is already glazed, I leave it out.

MAKES 24 BISCUITS

2 cups soft wheat self-rising flour

3 teaspoons sugar (optional)

4 tablespoons unsalted butter, cut into $1/2$-inch chunks and chilled for 15 minutes

$1/4$ cup vegetable shortening, cut into $1/2$-inch chunks and chilled for 15 minutes

$3/4$ cup whole buttermilk, plus more if needed

2 tablespoons cream

All-purpose flour for dusting

Melted butter for brushing the tops

Preheat the oven to 450°. Use a nonstick cake pan or baking sheet with a silicone liner.

Measure the flour into a large mixing bowl and whisk in the sugar, if desired. Add the cold chunks of butter. Using a pastry blender or your fingertips, break up the chunks a little, then add the shortening. Continue to break up the chunks until they're about the size of peas.

Make a well in the center and pour in the buttermilk and cream. Starting at the sides of the bowl, use a spatula or wooden spoon to toss the flour over the buttermilk. Continue to work in the flour from the sides of the bowl, just until the dough comes together.

If the dough starts to pull away from the sides of the bowl and sticks to your fingers, you have the right amount of buttermilk. If there are dry spots and the dough isn't sticky when you touch it, add more buttermilk.

Dust a surface with all-purpose flour and turn the dough out onto the surface. Flour your hands, then cuddle the dough by pressing your hands around the outer edges. Pat and press the top of the dough with your floured hands. Fold the dough in half, pat it, and fold it again. Repeat this two or three times until the outside of the dough feels less sticky and becomes smooth.

Use a rolling pin or pat the dough to flatten it ½ inch thick.

Cut the biscuits using a 1½-inch biscuit cutter without twisting the cutter. Place the biscuits in the cake pan or baking sheet so they touch if you like soft sides or about ½ inch apart for crisper sides.

Combine the leftover pieces of dough and cuddle them with your hands, handling the dough as little as possible. Cut more biscuits. Form the remaining scraps into a snake and place it around the biscuits. This will make the biscuits rise more evenly. (And the snake makes a crispy extra for the cook.)

Bake the biscuits in the center of the oven until they're light golden brown, 8–10 minutes. Brush the tops with melted butter.

High-Rise Biscuits,
a.k.a. Food-Processor Biscuits

One of the complaints about biscuit making that I hear most often is from people who say they can't make a biscuit that's tall enough. Want a really tall biscuit? Looking for a simple way to cut in shortening? Try using a mixer or food processor, but remember that when you add the liquid, as soon as the dough is wet stop mixing or you'll have a tough biscuit or a nice doorstop.

Since many restaurants use kitchen appliances as a shortcut to making biscuits, this is one of the secrets of a restaurant-style biscuit.

MAKES 12 BISCUITS

---

2 cups soft wheat self-rising flour

5 tablespoons vegetable shortening, unsalted butter, or lard, cut into ½-inch chunks and chilled for 15 minutes

¾ cup whole buttermilk, plus more if needed

2 tablespoons heavy cream

All-purpose flour for dusting

Melted butter for brushing the tops

Preheat the oven to 500°. Use a nonstick cake pan or baking sheet.

Measure the flour into the bowl of a food processor or stand mixer. Add the cold chunks of shortening, butter, or lard.

If using a food processor, pulse about 6 times. Use a spatula to stir the flour to see if the chunks are the size of peas. If they aren't, pulse a few more times and recheck.

If using a stand mixer, with the paddle blade attached, turn the mixer on low and mix for 1 minute. Use a spatula to stir the flour to see if the chunks are the size of peas. If they aren't, mix a bit longer and recheck.

Add about a third of the buttermilk at a time and the cream, pulsing after each addition in the food processor or stirring after each addition in the stand mixer. Once the dough is wet, stop. It's important not to overwork the dough.

Dust a surface with all-purpose flour and turn the dough out onto the surface. Flour your hands, then cuddle the dough by pressing your hands around the outer edges. Pat and press the top of the dough with your floured hands. Fold the dough in half, pat it, and fold it again. Repeat this two or three times until the outside of the dough feels less sticky and becomes smooth.

Use a rolling pin or pat the dough to flatten it to the desired thickness: ½ inch for traditional biscuits or up to 1 inch for very tall biscuits.

Cut the biscuits using a 2-inch biscuit cutter without twisting the cutter. Place the biscuits in the cake pan or baking sheet so they touch if you like soft sides or about a ½ inch apart for crisper sides.

Combine the leftover pieces of dough and cuddle them with your hands, handling the dough as little as possible. Cut more biscuits. Form the remaining scraps into a snake and place it around the biscuits. This will make the biscuits rise more evenly. (And the snake makes a crispy extra for the cook.)

Bake the biscuits in the center of the oven until they're light golden brown, 8–10 minutes. Brush the tops with melted butter.

Flaky Butter Biscuits

Are superflaky biscuits impossible to make from scratch? Can't a biscuit be as flaky and buttery as a croissant? Yes, it's all about layers. To create layers, fold the dough as in making puff pastry. The inspiration for this biscuit came from famed Charlotte-based cookbook author, bread baker, pastry chef, and Johnson and Wales instructor Peter Reinhardt. I love the results. These biscuits are so good that I serve them for Thanksgiving. I use all-purpose flour for this recipe to make the layers more pronounced.

MAKES 16–20 BISCUITS

1 stick unsalted butter

2 cups all-purpose flour, plus more for dusting

2½ teaspoons baking powder

1 teaspoon kosher salt

1 tablespoon sugar

1 cup heavy cream mixed with 1 tablespoon lemon juice
  (let stand for 10 minutes)

Melted butter for brushing the tops (optional)

Put the butter in the freezer for at least 30 minutes before you start baking to give it time to get very cold and hard. If you have the space in your freezer, freeze the flour too.

Preheat the oven to 450°. Use a baking sheet with a silicone liner.

Whisk together the flour, baking powder, salt, and sugar in a large mixing bowl. Place the mixture in the freezer for at least 30 minutes.

Grate the butter in a food processor using the grater attachment or with a hand grater. Place the grated butter in the freezer for 30 minutes.

Gently toss the butter into the flour using a wooden spoon. Add the acidified cream and stir just until blended. If you need more liquid for the dough to pull together into a ball, add a small amount of cream and stir. The dough should come together into a ball, but it won't be wet.

Turn the dough out onto a lightly floured surface. Using a rolling pin coated with flour, roll out to a 12- × 18-inch rectangle, about ⅛ inch thick. Fold the dough into thirds like folding a letter. Pick up the dough to keep it from sticking, and lightly flour the surface. Roll the dough again about ⅛ inch thick. Repeat folding the dough into thirds and rolling it three more times. If the dough sticks, use a bench knife to pick up the dough and fold it. Handle the dough as little as possible.

Cut the biscuits using a 1½-inch biscuit cutter or slice the dough into squares using a pizza cutter or bench knife. Place the biscuits on the baking sheet about a ½ inch apart so the sides brown.

Bake for 12–15 minutes, or until the tops are golden brown. Remove from the oven. If desired, brush the tops with melted butter.

Shirley's Touch-of-Grace Biscuits

Shirley Corriher, food scientist and James Beard Award–winning cookbook author, has made thousands of these biscuits using what she calls "my little bitty blast furnace." When Shirley makes biscuits, she tells stories, talks with her hands, and keeps a room laughing—all while her hands are caked in dough.

It has been an honor to travel and bake biscuits with her through the years (she shapes them and I put them in the oven). Sometimes when I make her recipe, I add sugar and sometimes I leave it out. Her biscuits are ultralight and run together like pull-apart rolls.

MAKES 12 BISCUITS

---

2 cups soft wheat self-rising flour

¼ cup sugar (optional)

½ teaspoon salt

¼ cup vegetable shortening, cut into ½-inch chunks and chilled for 15 minutes

⅔ cup cream

¾ cup whole buttermilk, plus more if needed

1 cup all-purpose flour

Melted butter for brushing the tops

Preheat the oven to 425°. Position a shelf slightly below the center of the oven. Coat a 9-inch cake pan with nonstick cooking spray.

Combine the flour, sugar (if desired), and salt in a large mixing bowl. Add the cold chunks of shortening and toss them in the flour to coat. Using a pastry blender or your fingertips, break up the chunks until they're about the size of peas.

Make a well in the center and gently stir in the cream, then add the buttermilk until the dough resembles cottage cheese. It should be a wet mess but not soupy.

Spread the all-purpose flour out on a plate or pie pan. With a medium ice cream scoop or spoon, place 3 scoops of dough at a time well apart in the flour. Sprinkle flour over each and flour your hands. Roll each biscuit in the flour to coat it, pick it up, then gently shape it into a ball, shaking off the excess flour as you work. Place the biscuits next to each other in the prepared cake pan.

Bake the biscuits until they're light golden brown, about 20–25 minutes. Brush the tops melted butter. Invert onto one plate, then back onto another. With a knife or spatula, cut between the biscuits to make them easy to remove.

John Egerton's Beaten Biscuits

John Egerton, historian and author of numerous books including Southern Food: At Home, on the Road, and in History, *was once spotted walking down the street in Nashville carrying what appeared to be an old sewing machine, complete with cast-iron legs, with a contraption that looked like a giant pasta machine mounted to the top. It turned out to be a machine called a biscuit break that was created by DeMuth to make beaten biscuits without having to beat them. Egerton is passing along the method and the machine to young chefs who are keeping the tradition alive.*

Beaten biscuits are the first biscuits, descendants of hardtack, the bread that kept many shipmen and warriors alive throughout the centuries. The "light" version of hardtack was beaten biscuits. Shortening, milk, flour, and a lot of hard work beating the dough went into making this biscuit.

In American Cookery *of 1796,* Amelia Simmon's recipe for "Biscuit" was "one pound flour, two ounces butter, one egg, wet with milk and break while oven is heating." The term "break" means to beat, specifically with an ax or rolling pin—in the antebellum South, a task performed by slaves or servants.*

John Egerton's family owned a biscuit break. The machine flattens the dough, and then the cook runs it through the machine again and again. "There's an old saying that you would beat the dough 100 times for family and 500 times for company," says Egerton.

Beaten biscuits are hard and cracker-like, perfect for sliced ham, so often where ham is eaten, beaten biscuits are still made. With a thin slice of great-quality country ham, these are a little bit of heaven. This recipe uses a food-processor method, not the same as using a biscuit break but the only way most of us have to make them at home short of bludgeoning them with an ax.

3½ cups soft wheat all-purpose flour
½ teaspoon baking powder
½ teaspoon fine sea salt
2 tablespoons sugar
½ cup lard
¾ cup very cold half-and-half

Use a baking sheet.

Whisk together the flour, baking powder, salt, and sugar in a large mixing bowl. Add the lard chunks and toss them in the flour to coat. Using a pastry blender or your fingertips, break up the chunks until they're about the size of peas.

Make a well in the center and gently stir in the half-and-half. Shape the dough into a ball and seal it in a plastic bag. Leave the dough on the counter for a few hours or overnight.

Preheat the oven to 325°.

Divide the dough in half and place each half in a food processor fitted with the dough blade for 2 minutes. Roll the dough ½ inch thick, fold it, and roll it again. Continue working the dough until it's very smooth, then roll it ½ inch thick.

Cut the biscuits using a 2-inch biscuit cutter without twisting the cutter. Place the biscuits on the baking sheet ½ inch apart, and pierce each biscuit three times with a fork.

Bake for 5 minutes on the bottom rack of the oven, then move to the center rack and bake for 25 minutes. The biscuits are done when they're light tan, firm on the outside, and dry and flaky on the inside. Serve warm or cold with tissue-thin slices of ham.

Lynn's Paradise Café's Pan Biscuits

You don't come to Lynn's Paradise Café in the old Highlands neighborhood of Louisville, Kentucky, for the biscuits; you come for the seasonal and creative breakfast. But the biscuits are memorable too. Owner Lynn Winter beat Bobby Flay in a Breakfast Throwdown and has been written up in many food magazines. So when I phoned to ask for her recipe, I expected the response to be "no." Instead, I had the recipe within an hour, but then that's the type of service I remember when I used to frequent the restaurant.

You always have fun at Lynn's. First there's the funky décor. My daughter loved to play with the toys on every table, the giant pigs, the teapot water fountains, and the eggs hanging on the tree in the dining room.

Then there's the food. Since the restaurant is known for its breakfast, it must make thousands of biscuits every day. They come to the table as big chunks of biscuit, tall and light. They're rarely the star of the plate, usually overshadowed by one of Lynn's inventive main courses, such as BLT fries with spinach and horseradish sour cream or a three-egg omelet filled with something delicious from a local farm.

The biscuits are simple to make because you press the dough into the pan. They're buttery, tender bites to go alongside whatever dish you're inspired to create.

MAKES 9 OR 16 BISCUITS

---

4 cups soft wheat flour

4 teaspoons baking powder

1 teaspoon baking soda

1¼ teaspoons salt

⅔ cup vegetable shortening, cut into ½-inch chunks and chilled for 15 minutes

1½ cups buttermilk

1 cup heavy cream

Melted butter for brushing the tops

Preheat the oven to 425°. Coat a 9-inch square baking pan with nonstick cooking spray.

Whisk together the flour, baking powder, baking soda, and salt in a large mixing bowl. Add the cold chunks of shortening. Using a pastry blender, cut up the chunks until they're about the size of peas.

Make a well in the center and pour in the buttermilk and cream. Starting at the sides of the bowl, use a spatula or wooden spoon to toss the flour over the buttermilk. Continue to work in the flour from the sides of the bowl, just until mixed.

The dough will be very wet and sticky. Turn the dough out into the prepared baking pan and use a spatula or spoon to spread it evenly. Dust your hands with flour and lightly pat the dough until it's even and pressed into the corners.

Using a floured bench knife or table knife, cut through the dough to make 9 or 16 square biscuits. Brush the tops with melted butter.

Bake for 30–35 minutes. To test for doneness, lightly press the top of one of the center biscuits with your finger. If the biscuit springs back, they're done. If it doesn't, bake for another 5 minutes and test again. Remove the biscuits from the oven and let them rest 5 minutes before removing them from the pan. Turn the biscuits out of the pan and cut into squares.

Buttermilk-Butter
Food Truck Biscuits

A food truck aptly named Farm Truck parks each Saturday at the Knoxville, Tennessee, Market Square Farmers' Market and offers biscuits and then later, dreamy ice cream. With a red bandanna covering her head, Colleen Cruze skims off the top of her father Earl's famous Cruze Dairy buttermilk and butter to make her biscuits.

Cruze Dairy doesn't ship, but if you find yourself in eastern Tennessee, look for this buttermilk. The famed chef of The French Laundry, Thomas Keller, is among many others who've made a pilgrimage to the farm. Joe York even made a film about Earl Cruze for the Southern Foodways Alliance.

I decided to make my own version of Colleen's recipe using half butter and half buttermilk. Most of us can't get the amazing buttermilk from the eastern Tennessee farm, so I did my best to approximate the recipe. If you can't use Cruze Dairy buttermilk, at least you have a recipe with over-the-top buttery buttermilk flavor.

MAKES ABOUT 4 BISCUITS

1½ cups soft wheat self-rising flour
12 tablespoons unsalted butter, at room temperature
¾ cup whole buttermilk, plus more if needed
All-purpose flour for dusting
Melted butter for brushing the tops

Preheat the oven to 500°. Use a nonstick cake pan or baking sheet.

Measure the flour into a large mixing bowl.

In a small bowl, stir together the butter and buttermilk using a wooden spoon. The butter won't become incorporated into the buttermilk but will remain lumpy.

Make a well in the center and pour in ¾ of the buttermilk mixture. Starting at the sides of the bowl, use a spatula or wooden spoon to toss the flour over the buttermilk. Continue to work in the flour from the sides of the bowl, just until the dough comes together.

If the dough starts to pull away from the sides of the bowl and sticks to your fingers, you have the right amount of buttermilk. If there are dry spots and the dough isn't sticky when you touch it, add more buttermilk.

Dust a surface with all-purpose flour and turn the dough out onto the surface. Flour your hands, then cuddle the dough by pressing your hands around the outer edges. Pat and press the top of the dough with your floured hands. Fold the dough in half, pat it, and fold it again. Repeat this two or three times until the outside of the dough feels less sticky and becomes smooth.

Use a rolling pin or pat the dough to flatten it to the desired thickness: ½ inch for traditional biscuits or up to 1 inch for very tall biscuits.

Cut the biscuits using a 3-inch biscuit cutter without twisting the cutter. Place the biscuits in the cake pan or baking sheet so they touch if you like soft sides or about ½ inch apart for crisper sides.

Combine the leftover pieces of dough and cuddle them with your hands, handling the dough as little as possible. Cut more biscuits. Form the remaining scraps into a snake and place it around the biscuits. This will make the biscuits rise more evenly. (And the snake makes a crispy extra for the cook.)

Bake the biscuits in the center of the oven until they're light golden brown, 8–10 minutes. Brush the tops with melted butter.

Creamy Cream Cheese Biscuits

Inspired by the famed Callie's Charleston Biscuits, these are cheese biscuits with ham baked in the center, ready to eat. They freeze well and can be quickly prepared as a party appetizer by heating them at 350° in aluminum foil for about twenty minutes.

MAKES 24 BISCUITS

FOR THE FILLING

1½ cups chopped cooked ham
4 tablespoons unsalted butter, at room temperature
2 teaspoons honey

FOR THE BISCUITS

2 cups soft wheat self-rising flour
4 tablespoons unsalted butter, cut into ½-inch chunks and
chilled for 15 minutes
2 ounces cream cheese, cut into ½-inch chunks and chilled
for 15 minutes
½ cup shredded cheddar cheese
⅓ cup whole milk, plus more if needed
1 teaspoon prepared mustard
All-purpose flour for dusting
Melted butter for brushing the tops

Preheat the oven to 450°. Use a nonstick cake pan or baking sheet.

To make the filling, finely chop the ham using a food processor or a knife. Add the butter and honey by pulsing the food processor or mixing the ingredients in a bowl. Set aside.

To make the biscuits, measure the flour into a large mixing bowl. Add the cold chunks of butter and cream cheese and toss them in the flour to coat. Using a pastry blender or your fingertips, break up the chunks until they're about the size of peas.

Stir in the cheddar cheese.

Combine the milk and mustard in a small bowl.

Make a well in the center of the flour mixture and pour in the milk mixture. Starting at the sides of the bowl, use a spatula or wooden spoon to toss the flour over the milk. Continue to work in the flour from the sides of the bowl, just until the dough comes together.

If the dough starts to pull away from the sides of the bowl and sticks to your fingers, you have the right amount of milk. If there are dry spots and the dough isn't sticky when you touch it, add more milk.

Dust a surface with all-purpose flour and turn the dough out onto the surface. Flour your hands, then cuddle the dough by pressing your hands around the outer edges. Pat and press the top of the dough with your floured hands. Fold the dough in half, pat it, and fold it again. Repeat this two or three times until the outside of the dough feels less sticky and becomes smooth.

Use a rolling pin to flatten the dough into a rectangle a bit more than ⅛ inch thick. Cut the dough in half. Spread the ham mixture on half of the dough and then place the other half on top.

Using a bench knife, cut the biscuits into 1-inch squares. Place the biscuits in the cake pan or baking sheet so they touch if you like soft sides or about ½ inch apart for crisper sides.

Bake the biscuits in the center of the oven until they're light golden brown, 8–10 minutes. Brush the tops with melted butter.

Flavored Biscuits

A LITTLE SOMETHING MORE

It's hard to beat a simple biscuit with butter, but then there's cheese. Not to mention herbs and fruits and spices. The biscuits in the last chapter featured slight changes in the ingredients or techniques that create different textures and flavors. This chapter is about taking those biscuits to new heights. It includes old-fashioned recipes that have been made for years and crazy new combos.

Recipes are just the starting point—use these recipes as a base to bake the flavors you enjoy in biscuit form. I've discovered some of my favorite combinations because they were the ingredients that I happened to have in my pantry at the time. Add what you like to a biscuit—the results will astound you and become signature appetizers, dinner breads, or the centerpiece for breakfast.

Cheese Straws

I was babysitting my eighteen-month-old niece, Abigail. We were rocking along just fine for a while, but then she started to get fussy, so I did what any aunt would do—I found her something to eat. Like magic, she was soothed by little cheese crackers that I had cut into heart shapes.

Later, I was making a quick appetizer of cheese straws for a family gathering that included my brother David, Abigail's father. He loved these and couldn't stop eating them. These cheese straws are my best babysitting trick and party appetizer all rolled into one recipe.

MAKES ABOUT 2 DOZEN CHEESE STRAWS,
depending on size

3/4 cup all-purpose flour

1/8 teaspoon cayenne pepper

1/2 teaspoon salt

1 1/2 cups shredded cheddar cheese

4 tablespoons unsalted butter, cut into 1/2-inch chunks and chilled for 15 minutes

1 tablespoon cream

All-purpose flour for dusting

Preheat the oven to 350°. Use a baking sheet or nonstick cake pan.

Whisk together the flour, cayenne pepper, and salt in a large mixing bowl. Add the cheese and cold chunks of butter and toss them in the flour to coat. Using a pastry blender or your fingertips, break up the chunks until they're about the size of peas.

Make a well in the center and pour in the cream. Starting at the sides of the bowl, use a spatula or wooden spoon to toss the flour over the cream. Continue to work in the flour from the sides of the bowl, just until the dough comes together.

Dust a surface with all-purpose flour and turn the dough out onto the surface. Flour your hands, then cuddle the dough by pressing your hands around the outer edges. Pat and press the top of the dough with your floured hands. Fold the dough in half, pat it, and fold it again. Repeat this two or three times until the outside of the dough feels less sticky and becomes smooth.

Use a rolling pin or pat the dough to flatten it ⅛ inch thick to make a 9-inch square. Cut the dough into strips about ¼ inch wide and 4½ inches long or use a 1-inch biscuit cutter to cut the dough into rounds. Place the cheese straws on the baking sheet about ½ inch apart for crisper sides. If making biscuits, place ½ inch apart in the cake pan or baking sheet and use a fork to prick a few holes in the top so they don't puff up.

Combine the leftover pieces of dough and cuddle them with your hands, handling the dough as little as possible. Cut more straws or biscuits.

Bake the straws or biscuits in the center of the oven until they're light golden brown, 10–12 minutes. Move to a cooling rack to cool completely.

Gorgonzola, Walnut, and Cranberry Biscuits

These sweet, salty, tangy, crispy bites are colorful, easy-to-make little drop biscuits. I add whatever I have on hand. Use a strong-flavored cheese, nuts, and raisins or other dried fruit to create your own combination.

MAKES ABOUT 24 BISCUITS

---

2 cups soft wheat self-rising flour

1½ tablespoons sugar

5⅓ tablespoons unsalted butter, cut into ½-inch chunks and chilled for 15 minutes

8 ounces Gorgonzola cheese, crumbled

1 cup chopped toasted walnuts

1 cup diced dried cranberries

¾ cup whole buttermilk, plus more if needed

Melted butter for brushing the tops

Preheat the oven to 450°. Use a nonstick cake pan or baking sheet.

Whisk together the flour and sugar in a large mixing bowl. Add the cold chunks of butter and toss them in the flour to coat. Using a pastry blender or your fingertips, break up the chunks until they're about the size of peas.

Stir in the cheese, walnuts, and dried cranberries. Make a well in the center and pour in the buttermilk. Starting at the sides of the bowl, use a spatula or wooden spoon to toss the flour over the buttermilk. Continue to work in the flour from the sides of the bowl, just until the dough comes together.

If the dough starts to pull away from the sides of the bowl and sticks to your fingers, you have the right amount of buttermilk. If there are dry spots and the dough isn't sticky when you touch it, add more buttermilk.

Using a small cookie scoop or heaping teaspoon, drop the biscuits onto the cake pan or baking sheet about ½ inch apart. Bake the biscuits in the center of the oven until they're light golden brown, 8–10 minutes. Brush the tops with melted butter.

Orange Tea Biscuits

This biscuit was served with a salad at the Inn at Blackberry Farm in eastern Tennessee using a recipe from John Martin Taylor's Hoppin' John's Lowcountry Cooking. *The view of the Smoky Mountains from this beautiful inn and the biscuit made with fresh, sweet orange juice made the meal a memorable experience. It was brunch-biscuit perfection.*

My adaptation of the recipe makes a small buttery biscuit just waiting for coffee or tea so you can slow down and enjoy your morning wherever you may be. It works well with lemon instead of orange if you like.

MAKES 12 BISCUITS

---

12 sugar cubes

Juice from 1 orange

2 cups soft wheat self-rising flour

1 tablespoon sugar

$\frac{1}{4}$ cup vegetable shortening, unsalted butter, or lard, cut into $\frac{1}{2}$-inch chunks and chilled for 15 minutes

$\frac{3}{4}$ cup whole buttermilk or milk, plus more if needed

All-purpose flour for dusting

Melted butter for brushing the tops

1 teaspoon grated orange zest

Preheat the oven to 450°. Use a nonstick cake pan or baking sheet with a silicone liner.

Soak the sugar cubes in the orange juice while making the biscuits.

Whisk together the flour and sugar in a large mixing bowl. Add the cold chunks of shortening, butter, or lard and toss them in the flour to coat. Using a pastry blender or your fingertips, break up the chunks until they're about the size of peas.

Make a well in the center and pour in the buttermilk or milk. Starting at the sides of the bowl, use a spatula or wooden spoon to toss the flour over the buttermilk. Continue to work in the flour from the sides of the bowl, just until the dough comes together.

If the dough starts to pull away from the sides of the bowl and sticks to your fingers, you have the right amount of buttermilk. If there are dry spots and the dough isn't sticky when you touch it, add more buttermilk.

Dust a surface with all-purpose flour and turn the dough out onto the surface. Flour your hands, then cuddle the dough by pressing your hands around the outer edges. Pat and press the top of the dough with your floured hands. Fold the dough in half, pat it, and fold it again. Repeat this two or three times until the outside of the dough feels less sticky and becomes smooth.

Use a rolling pin or pat the dough to flatten it between ¼ inch and ½ inch thick.

Cut the biscuits using a 2-inch biscuit cutter without twisting the cutter. Place the biscuits in the cake pan or baking sheet so they touch if you like soft sides or about ½ inch apart for crisper sides.

Combine the leftover pieces of dough and cuddle them with your hands, handling the dough as little as possible. Cut more biscuits. Form the remaining scraps into a snake and place it around the biscuits. This will make the biscuits rise more evenly. (And the snake makes a crispy extra for the cook.)

Press an orange-juice-soaked sugar cube into each biscuit. Brush the tops with melted butter and sprinkle evenly with the orange zest.

Bake the biscuits in the center of the oven until they're light golden brown, 8–10 minutes. Brush the tops with melted butter.

My Favorite Sweet Potato Biscuits

You might picture these biscuits nestled in one of your best white napkins on your Thanksgiving table, but don't limit them to the one day we think of eating sweet potatoes. A little sweet and cinnamon-spiced, these are breakfast-biscuit or ham-biscuit worthy any day.

Even though they seem to be a special-occasion biscuit, historically that wasn't the case. Sweet potatoes were plentiful in the southern states during the Civil War, but flour and sugar were in short supply. Enslaved West Africans knew from their food traditions that tubers can be used to replace flour, so they used sweet potatoes to make bread and pies with less sugar and flour. Sweet potatoes were survival food.

This is one of my favorite recipes for fall and winter, when sweet potatoes are plentiful.

MAKES 12 BISCUITS

1 cup soft wheat self-rising flour

¼ teaspoon ground cinnamon

2 tablespoons firmly packed brown sugar

½ teaspoon baking powder

4 tablespoons unsalted butter, cut into ½-inch chunks and chilled for 15 minutes

¾ cup cooked, mashed sweet potatoes

All-purpose flour for dusting

Melted butter for brushing the tops

Preheat the oven to 425°. Use a nonstick cake pan or baking sheet.

Whisk together the flour, cinnamon, brown sugar, and baking powder in a large mixing bowl. Add the cold chunks of butter and toss them in the flour to coat. Using a pastry blender or your fingertips, break up the chunks until they're about the size of peas.

Make a well in the center and add the sweet potatoes. Starting at the sides of the bowl, use a spatula or wooden spoon to toss the flour over the sweet potatoes. Continue to work in the flour from the sides of the bowl, just until the dough comes together. The dough will be sticky.

Dust a surface with all-purpose flour and turn the dough out onto the surface. Flour your hands, then cuddle the dough by pressing your hands around the outer edges. Pat and press the top of the dough with your floured hands. Fold the dough in half, pat it, and fold it again. Repeat this two or three times until the outside of the dough feels less sticky and becomes smooth.

Use a rolling pin or pat the dough to flatten it to the desired thickness: ½ inch for traditional biscuits or up to 1 inch for very tall biscuits.

Cut the biscuits using a 2-inch biscuit cutter without twisting the cutter. Place the biscuits in the cake pan or baking sheet so they touch if you like soft sides or about ½ inch apart for crisper sides.

Combine the leftover pieces of dough and cuddle them with your hands, handling the dough as little as possible. Cut more biscuits. Form the remaining scraps into a snake and place it around the biscuits. This will make the biscuits rise more evenly. (And the snake makes a crispy extra for the cook.)

Bake the biscuits in the center of the oven until they're light golden brown, 10–12 minutes. Brush the tops with melted butter.

Mayonnaise Biscuits

When I first found these biscuits in a 1960s cookbook, I laughed. I put them in the same category as TV dinners and Jell-O molds. The drawing on the cover of a woman wearing pearls and an apron didn't inspire me either.

But I didn't forget about the recipe. I had to try it, but with no expectations that the biscuits would be good. Now I don't really know why I ever thought the idea was so strange. Eggs, lemon, and oil aren't uncommon ingredients in bread, so why not use mayonnaise and save a few steps? This is a throwback worth keeping, but no need for the pearls.

MAKES 16 BISCUITS

2 cups soft wheat self-rising flour
6 tablespoons mayonnaise
⅔ cup whole milk, plus more if needed
All-purpose flour for dusting
Melted butter for brushing the tops

Preheat the oven to 450°. Use a nonstick cake pan or baking sheet.

Measure the flour into a large mixing bowl.

Make a well in the center, spoon in the mayonnaise, and pour in the milk. Starting at the sides of the bowl, use a spatula or wooden spoon to toss the flour over the milk. Continue to work in the flour from the sides of the bowl, just until the dough comes together.

If the dough starts to pull away from the sides of the bowl and sticks to your fingers, you have the right amount of milk. If there are dry spots and the dough isn't sticky when you touch it, add more milk.

Dust a surface with all-purpose flour and turn the dough out onto the surface. Flour your hands, then cuddle the dough by pressing your hands around the outer edges. Pat and press the top of the dough with your floured hands. Fold the dough in half, pat it, and fold it again. Repeat this two or three times until the outside of the dough feels less sticky and becomes smooth.

Use a rolling pin or pat the dough to flatten it to the desired thickness: ½ inch for traditional biscuits or up to 1 inch for very tall biscuits.

Cut the biscuits using a 1½-inch biscuit cutter without twisting the cutter. Place the biscuits in the cake pan or baking sheet so they touch if you like soft sides or about ½ inch apart for crisper sides.

Combine the leftover pieces of dough and cuddle them with your hands, handling the dough as little as possible. Cut more biscuits. Form the remaining scraps into a snake and place it around the biscuits. This will make the biscuits rise more evenly. (And the snake makes a crispy extra for the cook.)

Bake the biscuits in the center of the oven until they're light golden brown, 8–10 minutes. Brush the tops with melted butter.

Fresh Garlic, Cheese, and Herb Biscuits

If I don't have fresh garlic on hand, I can't cook. So it's natural that I think that all it takes to make a dinner biscuit is to brush it with garlic butter. And it seems most everyone agrees.

For this biscuit, I tossed in a terrific Italian seasoning blend, but I often use a mixture of fresh herbs from my garden. If you're using fresh herbs, use any combination you like. Try thyme, rosemary, and chives, chopped fine.

MAKES 8 BISCUITS

FOR THE BISCUITS

2 cups soft wheat self-rising flour

4 tablespoons unsalted butter, cut into ½-inch chunks and chilled for 15 minutes

1 cup shredded cheddar cheese

1 tablespoon good-quality Italian seasoning or 3 tablespoons fresh herbs

¾ cup whole milk, plus more if needed

FOR THE GARLIC BUTTER

4 tablespoons unsalted butter

1 clove garlic, minced

2 tablespoons finely chopped parsley

Salt to taste

Preheat the oven to 450°. Use a nonstick cake pan or baking sheet.

Measure the flour into a large mixing bowl. Add the cold chunks of butter and toss them in the flour to coat. Using a pastry blender or your fingertips, break up the chunks until they're about the size of peas.

Stir in the cheese and Italian seasoning or fresh herbs.

Make a well in the center and pour in the milk. Starting at the sides of the bowl, use a spatula or wooden spoon to toss the flour over the milk. Continue to work in the flour from the sides of the bowl, just until the dough comes together.

If the dough starts to pull away from the sides of the bowl and sticks to your fingers, you have the right amount of milk. If there are dry spots and the dough isn't sticky when you touch it, add more milk.

Using an ice cream scoop or heaping tablespoon, drop the biscuits onto the cake pan or baking sheet. Since these biscuits are crisp, drop each scoop about ½ inch apart.

Bake the biscuits in the center of the oven until they're light golden brown, 8–10 minutes.

To make the garlic butter, melt the butter in a small sauté pan. Stir in the garlic and cook for about 30 seconds. Add the parsley and salt to taste. Brush the tops of the biscuits with garlic butter.

Pimento Cheese Biscuits

2011 was the year of pimento cheese, according to Adam Rapoport in Bon Appétit, *but southerners have always thought it was in vogue. Besides eating it in sandwiches, we slather it on celery sticks, burgers, and potatoes. In 2011, though, pimento cheese became the "new" ingredient and traveled beyond the South, according to pimento cheese expert Emily Wallace. (She actually wrote her master's thesis at the University of North Carolina on pimento cheese.) She discovered pimento cheese sushi, pimento cheese cheesecake, and the list goes on. After hearing a presentation by Emily at a Southern Foodways Alliance annual meeting, I decided to try my hand at pimento cheese biscuits. Why not combine two southern favorites? I would serve these on any occasion you would serve pimento cheese, which to me means anytime, but especially at parties.*

MAKES ABOUT 12 BISCUITS

2 cups soft wheat self-rising flour

2 teaspoons sugar

1 teaspoon freshly ground black pepper

$\frac{1}{4}$ teaspoon cayenne pepper

$\frac{1}{4}$ cup mayonnaise

1 cup whole milk

1 cup shredded sharp cheddar cheese

2 tablespoons diced pimentos

Melted butter for brushing the tops (optional)

Heat the oven to 450°. Coat a baking sheet with nonstick spray.

Whisk together the flour, sugar, black pepper, and cayenne pepper in a large mixing bowl. Stir in the mayonnaise and milk until the flour is moistened. Stir in the cheese and pimentos.

Drop by heaping tablespoons onto the prepared baking sheet about 2 inches apart.

Bake for 10–12 minutes, or until golden brown.

If desired, brush the tops with melted butter.

Everything Biscuits

I'm smitten with these biscuits, one of my favorite busy weekday-morning meals. The strategy to making them is to make a big weekend breakfast, being sure to make enough for leftovers. Wow them with eggs, bacon, and sausage, then take the leftovers and make Everything Biscuits. Let the biscuits cool, wrap individual servings, and store them in the freezer. Pop them in the microwave when you're ready to eat. You'll have breakfast covered for the rest of week.

MAKES ABOUT 12 BIG BISCUITS

3 large eggs

1 tablespoon unsalted butter

1 tablespoon cream cheese

6 slices bacon

$\frac{1}{2}$ pound bulk breakfast sausage

$1\frac{1}{2}$ cups soft wheat self-rising flour

$\frac{1}{4}$ cup shortening or rendered bacon fat, cut into
$\frac{1}{2}$-inch chunks and chilled for 15 minutes

1 cup shredded cheddar cheese

$\frac{1}{2}$ cup milk, plus more if needed

Preheat the oven to 450°. Use a baking sheet.

Beat the eggs in a small bowl. Melt the butter in a skillet over medium heat and add the eggs. Cook the eggs slowly, folding the cooked part of the eggs with the uncooked eggs. When the eggs start to cook, fold in the cream cheese. Break up into small chunks and set aside.

In another skillet over medium heat, cook the bacon until crisp. Drain on paper towels and crumble into small pieces.

In the same skillet, cook the sausage, breaking up the pieces. Drain on paper towels.

Measure the flour into a large mixing bowl. Add the cold chunks of shortening or bacon fat and toss them in the flour to coat. Using a pastry blender or your fingertips, break up the chunks until they're about the size of peas.

Stir in the cooked eggs, bacon, sausage, and cheddar cheese. Make a well in the center and pour in the milk. Starting at the sides of the bowl, use a spatula or wooden spoon to toss the flour over the milk. Continue to work in the flour from the sides of the bowl, just until the dough comes together.

If the dough starts to pull away from the sides of the bowl and sticks to your fingers, you have the right amount of milk. If there are dry spots and the dough isn't sticky when you touch it, add more milk.

Use a ⅓-cup measure to drop the biscuits onto the baking sheet.

Bake until golden brown, about 16–18 minutes.

Pancetta, Rosemary, and Olive Oil Biscuits

Bacon in any form goes well with biscuits, but I especially like pancetta because it isn't cured. Add fresh rosemary and Parmigiano-Reggiano cheese. This biscuit is good with any meal, Italian or not.

MAKES ABOUT 12 BISCUITS

¼ pound pancetta
2 cups soft wheat self-rising flour
4 tablespoons unsalted butter, cut into ½-inch chunks and
    chilled for 15 minutes
½ cup shredded Parmigiano-Reggiano cheese
Pinch of finely chopped fresh rosemary
¼ cup whole milk, plus more if needed
2 tablespoons extra-virgin olive oil
All-purpose flour for dusting
Melted butter for brushing the tops

Preheat the oven to 500°. Use a nonstick cake pan or baking sheet.

Dice the pancetta and cook in a skillet over low heat until crisp. Drain on paper towels.

Measure the flour into a large mixing bowl. Add the cold chunks of butter and toss them in the flour to coat. Using a pastry blender or your fingertips, break up the chunks until they're about the size of peas.

Stir in the cheese and rosemary. Combine the milk and olive oil in a small bowl. Make a well in the center of the flour mixture and pour in the milk mixture. Starting at the sides of the bowl, use a spatula or wooden spoon to toss the flour over the milk. Continue to work in the flour from the sides of the bowl, just until the dough comes together.

If the dough starts to pull away from the sides of the bowl and sticks to your fingers, you have the right amount of milk. If there are dry spots and the dough isn't sticky when you touch it, add more milk.

Dust a surface with all-purpose flour and turn the dough out onto the surface. Flour your hands, then cuddle the dough by pressing your hands around the outer edges. Pat and press the top of the dough with your floured hands. Fold the dough in half, pat it, and fold it again. Repeat this two or three times until the outside of the dough feels less sticky and becomes smooth.

Use a rolling pin or pat the dough to flatten it to the desired thickness: ½ inch for traditional biscuits or up to 1 inch for very tall biscuits.

Cut the biscuits using a 2-inch biscuit cutter without twisting the cutter. Place the biscuits in the cake pan or baking sheet so they touch if you like soft sides or about ½ inch apart for crisper sides.

Combine the leftover pieces of dough and cuddle them with your hands, handling the dough as little as possible. Cut more biscuits. Form the remaining scraps into a snake and place it around the biscuits. This will make the biscuits rise more evenly. (And the snake makes a crispy extra for the cook.)

Bake the biscuits in the center of the oven until they're light golden brown, 8–10 minutes. Brush the tops with melted butter.

You-Can't-Call-This-a-Biscuit 100% Whole Wheat Biscuits

"That's darn good!" was the reaction of a friend who has diabetes but wants to enjoy good old southern food after eating one of these biscuits. The biscuits are hearty, nutty, and surprisingly good. While it could be argued that these aren't really biscuits (no one in my memory has a grandmother who used whole wheat), they're a way to get some whole grain on the breakfast table, and they're, well, darn good. If you aren't ready to go with all whole wheat, try half whole wheat flour and half soft wheat flour.

MAKES 6 BISCUITS

2 cups whole wheat pastry flour

1 tablespoon baking powder

1 teaspoon salt

2 tablespoons sugar

¾ cup milk or buttermilk, plus more if needed

⅓ cup light olive oil

Melted butter for brushing the tops

Preheat the oven to 450°. Use a nonstick cake pan or baking sheet.

Measure the flour into a large mixing bowl. Whisk in the baking powder, salt, and sugar. Mix together the milk or buttermilk and olive oil in a small bowl. Make a well in the center of the flour mixture and pour in the milk or buttermilk and olive oil. Starting at the sides of the bowl, use a spatula or wooden spoon to toss the flour over the milk. Continue to work in the flour from the sides of the bowl, just until the dough comes together.

If the dough starts to pull away from the sides of the bowl and sticks to your fingers, you have the right amount of milk. If there are dry spots and the dough isn't sticky when you touch it, add more milk.

Using an ice cream scoop or heaping tablespoon, drop the biscuits onto the cake pan or baking sheet. Since these biscuits are crisp, drop each scoop about ½ inch apart.

Bake the biscuits in the center of the oven until they're light golden brown, 10–12 minutes. Brush the tops with melted butter.

Cornbread Biscuits

Since most of us love cornbread, adapting a cornbread recipe to biscuits just seems natural. These have a drier texture, all the better for sopping up chili or soup.

MAKES 12 BISCUITS

---

2 cups self-rising cornmeal

1/2 cup soft wheat self-rising flour

1/2 cup vegetable shortening, unsalted butter, or lard, cut into 1/2-inch chunks and chilled for 15 minutes

3/4 cup whole buttermilk, plus more if needed

All-purpose flour for dusting

Melted butter for brushing the tops

Preheat the oven to 425°. Use a nonstick cake pan or baking sheet.

Whisk together the cornmeal and flour in a large mixing bowl. Add the cold chunks of shortening, butter, or lard and toss them in the flour to coat. Using a pastry blender or your fingertips, break up the chunks until they're about the size of peas.

Make a well in the center and pour in the buttermilk. Starting at the sides of the bowl, use a spatula or wooden spoon to toss the flour over the buttermilk. Continue to work in the flour from the sides of the bowl, just until the dough comes together.

If the dough starts to pull away from the sides of the bowl and sticks to your fingers, you have the right amount of buttermilk. If there are dry spots and the dough isn't sticky when you touch it, add more buttermilk.

Dust a surface with all-purpose flour and turn the dough out onto the surface. Flour your hands, then cuddle the dough by pressing your hands around the outer edges. Pat and press the top of the dough with your floured hands. Fold the dough in half, pat it, and fold it again. Repeat this two or three times until the outside of the dough feels less sticky and becomes smooth.

Use a rolling pin or pat the dough to flatten it to the desired thickness: ½ inch for traditional biscuits or up to 1 inch for very tall biscuits.

Cut the biscuits using a 2-inch biscuit cutter without twisting the cutter. Place the biscuits in the cake pan or baking sheet so they touch if you like soft sides or about ½ inch apart for crisper sides.

Combine the leftover pieces of dough and cuddle them with your hands, handling the dough as little as possible. Cut more biscuits. Form the remaining scraps into a snake and place it around the biscuits. This will make the biscuits rise more evenly. (And the snake makes a crispy extra for the cook.)

Bake the biscuits in the center of the oven until they're light golden brown, 10–12 minutes. Brush the tops with melted butter.

Goat Cheese Biscuits

It seems at every farmers' market someone is selling goat cheese these days. I can't pass up the opportunity to buy artisanal goat cheese. I toss it in eggs for breakfast and make biscuits with it to go along with the fresh produce, eggs with bright orange yolks, and pastured meats I bring home from the market each week.

I switched to soft wheat all-purpose flour for this recipe because self-rising flour has a bit too much salt for the salty cheese.

MAKES 12 BISCUITS

2 cups soft wheat all-purpose flour

1 tablespoon baking powder

$\frac{1}{2}$ teaspoon salt

2 ounces goat cheese, crumbled

$\frac{1}{2}$ cup whole milk, plus more if needed

$\frac{1}{2}$ cup cream

All-purpose flour for dusting

Melted butter for brushing the tops

Preheat the oven to 500°. Use a nonstick cake pan or baking sheet.

Whisk together the flour, baking powder, and salt in a large mixing bowl. Toss the crumbled goat cheese in the flour to coat.

Make a well in the center and pour in the milk and cream. Starting at the sides of the bowl, use a spatula or wooden spoon to toss the flour over the milk. Continue to work in the flour from the sides of the bowl, just until the dough comes together.

If the dough starts to pull away from the sides of the bowl and sticks to your fingers, you have the right amount of milk. If there are dry spots and the dough isn't sticky when you touch it, add more milk.

Dust a surface with all-purpose flour and turn the dough out onto the surface. Flour your hands, then cuddle the dough by pressing your hands around the outer edges. Pat and press the top of the dough with your floured hands. Fold the dough in half, pat it, and fold it again. Repeat this two or three times until the outside of the dough feels less sticky and becomes smooth.

Use a rolling pin or pat the dough to flatten it to the desired thickness: ½ inch for traditional biscuits or up to 1 inch for very tall biscuits.

Cut the biscuits using a biscuit cutter without twisting the cutter. Place the biscuits in the cake pan or baking sheet so they touch if you like soft sides or about ½ inch apart for crisper sides.

Combine the leftover pieces of dough and cuddle them with your hands, handling the dough as little as possible. Cut more biscuits. Form the remaining scraps into a snake and place it around the biscuits. This will make the biscuits rise more evenly. (And the snake makes a crispy extra for the cook.)

Bake the biscuits in the center of the oven until they're light golden brown, 8–10 minutes. Brush the tops with melted butter.

Vegan "Buttermilk" Biscuits

Coming up with a menu for my vegan friends and my sister Pam is a challenge for me but one I enjoy. Some of my favorite dishes are vegan, and I've created many vegan variations of my own recipes.

It's easy to make vegan biscuits with soy milk and shortening.

MAKES 12 BISCUITS

¾ cup plain soy milk, plus more if needed

1 teaspoon lemon juice or white vinegar

2 cups soft wheat self-rising flour

5 tablespoons vegetable shortening, cut into ½-inch chunks
   and chilled for 15 minutes, or cold coconut oil

All-purpose flour for dusting

Preheat the oven to 500°. Use a nonstick cake pan or baking sheet.

Combine the soy milk and lemon juice or vinegar and set aside for about 10 minutes.

Measure the flour into a large mixing bowl. Add the cold chunks of shortening and toss them in the flour to coat. Using a pastry blender or your fingertips, break up the chunks until they're about the size of peas.

Make a well in the center and pour in the soy milk. Starting at the sides of the bowl, use a spatula or wooden spoon to toss the flour over the soy milk. Continue to work in the flour from the sides of the bowl, just until the dough comes together.

If the dough starts to pull away from the sides of the bowl and sticks to your fingers, you have the right amount of soy milk. If there are dry spots and the dough isn't sticky when you touch it, add more soy milk.

Dust a surface with all-purpose flour and turn the dough out onto the surface. Flour your hands, then cuddle the dough by pressing your hands around the outer edges. Pat and press the top of the dough with your floured hands. Fold the dough in half, pat it, and fold it again. Repeat this two or three times until the outside of the dough feels less sticky and becomes smooth.

Use a rolling pin or pat the dough to flatten it to the desired thickness: ½ inch for traditional biscuits or up to 1 inch for very tall biscuits.

Cut the biscuits using a 2-inch biscuit cutter without twisting the cutter. Place the biscuits in the cake pan or baking sheet so they touch if you like soft sides or about ½ inch apart for crisper sides.

Combine the leftover pieces of dough and cuddle them with your hands, handling the dough as little as possible. Cut more biscuits. Form the remaining scraps into a snake and place it around the biscuits. This will make the biscuits rise more evenly. (And the snake makes a crispy extra for the cook.)

Bake the biscuits in the center of the oven until they're light golden brown, 8–10 minutes.

Black Pepper–Sour Cream Biscuits

If you like buttermilk biscuits but never have buttermilk on hand, try sour cream. This recipe is from my friend Nina Swan-Kohler, who teaches cooking classes at her home in Iowa. Her addition of garlic-infused black pepper gives this a simple but flavorful twist. She admits that biscuit-making isn't a family tradition, but her substitution of sour cream for buttermilk is delicious.

MAKES 16 BISCUITS

3 cups soft wheat self-rising flour

¾ teaspoon garlic-infused black pepper

1 cup sour cream (not low-fat)

⅔ cup whole milk, plus more if needed

4 tablespoons melted unsalted butter

All-purpose flour for dusting

Melted butter for brushing the tops

Preheat the oven to 500°. Use a nonstick cake pan or baking sheet.

Whisk together the flour and pepper in a large mixing bowl.

Make a well in the center and add the sour cream, milk, and melted butter. Starting at the sides of the bowl, use a spatula or wooden spoon to toss the flour over the milk. Continue to work in the flour from the sides of the bowl, just until the dough comes together.

If the dough starts to pull away from the sides of the bowl and sticks to your fingers, you have the right amount of milk. If there are dry spots and the dough isn't sticky when you touch it, add more milk.

Dust a surface with all-purpose flour and turn the dough out onto the surface. Flour your hands, then cuddle the dough by pressing your hands around the outer edges. Pat and press the top of the dough with your floured hands. Fold the dough in half, pat it, and fold it again. Repeat this two or three times until the outside of the dough feels less sticky and becomes smooth.

Use a rolling pin or pat the dough to flatten it to the desired thickness: ½ inch for traditional biscuits or up to 1 inch for very tall biscuits.

Cut the biscuits using a 2½-inch biscuit cutter without twisting the cutter. Place the biscuits in the cake pan or baking sheet so they touch if you like soft sides or about ½ inch apart for crisper sides.

Combine the leftover pieces of dough and cuddle them with your hands, handling the dough as little as possible. Cut more biscuits. Form the remaining scraps into a snake and place it around the biscuits. This will make the biscuits rise more evenly. (And the snake makes a crispy extra for the cook.)

Bake the biscuits in the center of the oven until they're light golden brown, 8–10 minutes. Brush the tops with melted butter.

Bacon-Cheddar Biscuits

Why not put the bacon right in the biscuit? That way it doesn't slide out of the biscuit while you're eating it.

MAKES 8 BISCUITS

2 cups soft wheat all-purpose flour

1 tablespoon baking powder

$\frac{1}{2}$ teaspoon salt

2 tablespoons firmly packed brown sugar

$\frac{1}{2}$ teaspoon freshly ground black pepper

4 tablespoons unsalted butter, cut into $\frac{1}{2}$-inch chunks and chilled for 15 minutes

6–8 ounces smoky bacon

1 cup shredded sharp cheddar cheese, divided

$\frac{3}{4}$ cup buttermilk, plus more if needed

1 tablespoon rendered bacon fat

Preheat the oven to 425°. Use a baking sheet.

Whisk together the flour, baking powder, salt, brown sugar, and pepper in a large mixing bowl. Cut in the butter until it's the size of small peas.

In a skillet over low heat, cook the bacon until done. Drain on paper towels, reserving the rendered fat. Finely chop the bacon and return to the skillet. Cook over low heat until the bacon is crisp and most of the fat is rendered, about 7 minutes. Allow to cool slightly.

Stir the bacon and half of the cheese into the flour mixture. Add the buttermilk and rendered bacon fat and stir to combine. Add additional buttermilk if needed to create a sticky dough.

Using an ice cream scoop or heaping tablespoon, drop the biscuits onto the baking sheet. Sprinkle the remaining cheese on top.

Bake for 12 minutes, or until the biscuits are golden brown.

Biscuit Meals

EXCUSES TO HAVE BISCUITS FOR DINNER

If you grew up somewhere other than the South, you might think biscuits are just for breakfast. My family had them for any meal, as did almost everyone I knew while growing up in Knoxville. Pot pie meant a biscuit crust, and dumplings meant soft, thin pieces of biscuit dough dropped into chicken broth. I didn't know there were other kinds of dumplings until I got out of college. Biscuit breakfast sandwiches can also be considered a meal, as well as leftover biscuits used for lunch-time sandwiches along with pork chops or fried chicken.

In southern vernacular, biscuits are often just called bread. Yeast bread is called light bread, a loaf of bread, or rolls. It's like ordering tea in the South: everyone knows "tea" means iced tea with sugar. Order bread in some parts, and everyone knows that means a biscuit or maybe cornbread.

So it just makes sense to add some "bread" to any meal, even an international take on biscuits.

The Sandwich Biscuit

A great biscuit sandwich starts with a biscuit that doesn't fall apart as you eat it. Making a sturdy biscuit relies partly on technique and partly on ingredients.

In the 1980s, I learned that fast-food biscuits are made with hard thin shards of highly processed shortening that's not available to home cooks. Since then, I've had no desire to eat one. So when I wanted a recipe for a sandwich biscuit, I turned to natural fats and a technique that wouldn't be too time-consuming. I wanted a biscuit with buttery goodness that tastes so good it demands more attention than eating while you drive.

MAKES 6 LARGE BISCUITS

---

3 cups soft wheat all-purpose flour
1 tablespoon plus 1 teaspoon baking powder
2 sticks unsalted butter, cut into ½-inch chunks and
    chilled for 15 minutes
1 cup whole buttermilk
All-purpose flour for dusting

Preheat the oven to 450°. Use a baking sheet.

Whisk together the flour and baking powder in a large mixing bowl. Cut in the butter. Add the buttermilk. Turn out onto a lightly floured surface.

Using your hands, quickly pat the dough about ½ inch thick. Then, using a pastry knife, cut the dough into thirds and stack the three pieces. Pat the stack of dough ½ inch thick. Turn the dough 90° and repeat the cutting and stacking about 6 times. This makes the dough very flaky and sturdy.

After the last turn, pat the dough, then use the pastry knife to cut the biscuits into 3- to 4-inch squares. Place on the baking sheet ½ inch apart and bake for 18–20 minutes, or until the biscuits are brown and not doughy in the center.

The Ultimate Biscuit Sandwich

Top your biscuit with breakfast sausage, a sunny-side-up egg, gravy, bacon, ham, a pork chop, meatloaf, or pork tenderloin and add any type of cheese, chutney, jam, mustard, or hot sauce. Pile on your favorite toppers for the ultimate sandwich. Be sure to start with The Sandwich Biscuit (page 80) to hold everything together. The list could go on and on, but here are a few ideas to get you started thinking.

THE THUNDER ROAD

A hot sausage patty and pimento cheese.

THE BB (BIG BARBECUE) BISCUIT

Your favorite barbecue, topped with sauce and cole slaw.

THE BRISKET BISCUIT

Cooked beef brisket, topped with caramelized onions and horse-radish sauce.

THE CHOCOLATE ELVIS

Chocolate nut butter (either hazelnut, peanut, or almond), banana slices, and cooked bacon. For an open-faced version, top with chocolate gravy.

Belinda's "Big Nasty"

Robert Sterling at Hominy Grill in Charleston has set the bar high with a sandwich called the "Big Nasty." It's fried chicken, shredded cheese, and sausage gravy on a biscuit. While his version is delicious, I wanted to make mine with chicken gravy. I like to mix bacon fat with the oil for frying the chicken because it adds to the breakfast quality of the sandwich. Here's my "Big Nasty," worthy of serving any time of day.

MAKES 6 SANDWICHES

The Sandwich Biscuit (page 80)

FOR THE CHICKEN

1¼ pounds boneless, skinless chicken breasts
½ cup soft wheat all-purpose flour
Salt and freshly ground black pepper
¼ cup bacon fat (optional)
Peanut or canola oil

FOR THE GRAVY

¼ cup all-purpose flour
2 cups chicken broth
Salt and freshly ground black pepper

Butterfly the chicken breasts by laying a breast on a cutting board and, with the knife parallel to the cutting board, slicing through the thick part of the breast, stopping before you reach the other side. The breast will open like a book, and the meat will be even in thickness. Use a meat pounder or rolling pin to gently pound the breasts ¾ inch or less thick.

Cut the breasts into 3- or 4-inch squares, depending on the size of the biscuits you use.

Place the flour in a shallow pan. Season each breast generously with salt and pepper, then dip it in the flour and press to coat it completely. Place the chicken in one layer on a plate, put it in the refrigerator, and let it chill for about 15 minutes.

Add the bacon fat, if desired, to a large frying pan, then add enough peanut or canola oil to reach a depth of ¼ inch. Heat the oil over medium heat until it shimmers.

Recoat the chicken breasts in flour if needed, and then gently place the pieces in the hot oil. Cook until the edges begin to turn brown. Turn and cook until the internal temperature of the chicken reaches 165°. By using a kitchen thermometer, you'll have juicy chicken that's done but not overcooked.

Drain the chicken on a rack with a pan underneath.

To make the gravy, drain the oil from the pan, leaving the bits in the bottom and reserving the oil. Add 4 tablespoons of the cooking oil back to the pan. Stir in the flour and cook over medium heat until it starts to brown, about 5 minutes. Gradually add the chicken broth, stirring vigorously. Add salt and pepper to taste.

To assemble the sandwich, slice each biscuit in half horizontally. Place a chicken breast on the bottom half of the biscuit. Spoon the gravy over the chicken breast—you can add either a little bit of gravy so you can pick up the sandwich or a lot of gravy so it's an open-faced sandwich that you eat with a fork. Place the top of the biscuit on top of the gravy for a hand-held sandwich or lean it over the gravy for an open-faced sandwich.

VARIATION ❋ You can substitute honey or sorghum for the gravy. I could eat these every day.

The Southern Reuben

You may scoff at my southernized version of a reuben sandwich, especially if you're one of the lucky people just a few subway stops from a great New York deli. I don't expect to see this sandwich on any menu in New York City anytime soon, but to my mind, that's just the Big Apple's loss.

I've always been partial to a steamy reuben, piled high with corned beef, and like many visitors to New York, I would never visit without stopping by Katz's Deli at least once. So back home, I added my favorite reuben ingredients to a biscuit sandwich. I know I'm breaking some hard-and-fast rules because everyone knows you use Russian rye bread in a reuben, but I use rye biscuits instead. Don't laugh until you've tried 'em.

MAKES 4 SMALL SANDWICHES
or 2 New York–sized sandwiches

1 cup soft wheat all-purpose flour

½ cup rye flour

2 teaspoons baking powder

½ teaspoon salt

1½ teaspoons caraway seeds

¼ cup olive oil

½ cup whole milk, plus more if needed

All-purpose flour for dusting

Melted butter for brushing the tops

4 tablespoons Russian or Thousand Island dressing

½ cup well-drained sauerkraut

½ pound thinly sliced corned beef

4 slices Swiss cheese

Preheat the oven to 450°. Use a nonstick cake pan or baking sheet.

Whisk together the all-purpose flour, rye flour, baking powder, salt, and caraway seeds in a large mixing bowl.

Mix together the olive oil and milk in a small bowl. Make a well in the center of the flour mixture and add the olive oil and milk. Starting at the sides of the bowl, use a spatula or wooden spoon to toss the flour over the milk. Continue to work in the flour from the sides of the bowl, just until the dough comes together.

If the dough starts to pull away from the sides of the bowl and sticks to your fingers, you have the right amount of milk. If there are dry spots and the dough isn't sticky when you touch it, add more milk.

Dust a surface with all-purpose flour and turn the dough out onto the surface. Flour your hands, then cuddle the dough by pressing your hands around the outer edges. Pat and press the top of the dough with your floured hands. Fold the dough in half, pat it, and fold it again. Repeat this two or three times until the outside of the dough feels less sticky and becomes smooth.

Use a rolling pin or pat the dough ½ inch thick.

Cut the biscuits using a 3-inch biscuit cutter without twisting the cutter, or for large sandwiches, cut the dough in half with a bench knife, and then cut around the edges to make 2 large squares. Place the biscuits in the cake pan or baking sheet so they touch if you like soft sides or about ½ inch apart for crisper sides.

Bake the biscuits in the center of the oven until they're light golden brown, 15–20 minutes. Brush the tops with melted butter.

To assemble the sandwich, slice each biscuit in half horizontally once the biscuits have cooled slightly. Spread dressing on each cut side, then place sauerkraut, corned beef, and a slice of Swiss cheese on the bottom half of the biscuit. Top with the other half, dressing-side down.

Butter the outside of the biscuits and place them in a skillet over medium-high heat, cover with a lid, and cook to brown the outside and melt the cheese, turning once.

VARIATION ❋ To make a breakfast reuben, add a fried egg.

Benne Seed Biscuits
with Pimento Cheese

Sesame seeds, believed to have been brought to colonial America by West African slaves as benne seeds, make a crisp biscuit that, when filled with pimento cheese, is a party favorite. Make them small so they'll go around a couple of times.

MAKES 24 BISCUITS

2 cups soft wheat all-purpose flour

2 teaspoons baking powder

$\frac{1}{2}$ teaspoon baking soda

1 teaspoon kosher salt

$\frac{1}{2}$ teaspoon cayenne pepper

$\frac{1}{2}$ cup toasted benne or sesame seeds

$\frac{1}{3}$ cup vegetable shortening, unsalted butter, or lard,
cut into $\frac{1}{2}$-inch chunks and chilled for 15 minutes

$\frac{1}{2}$ cup buttermilk, plus more if needed

All-purpose flour for dusting

2 cups prepared pimento cheese

Preheat the oven to 425°. Use a nonstick cake pan or baking sheet.

Whisk together the flour, baking powder, baking soda, salt, cayenne pepper, and benne seeds in a large mixing bowl. Add the cold chunks of shortening, butter, or lard and toss them in the flour to coat. Using a pastry blender or your fingertips, break up the chunks until they're about the size of peas.

Make a well in the center and pour in the buttermilk. Starting at the sides of the bowl, use a spatula or wooden spoon to toss the flour over the buttermilk. Continue to work in the flour from the sides of the bowl, just until the dough comes together.

If the dough starts to pull away from the sides of the bowl and sticks to your fingers, you have the right amount of buttermilk. If there are dry spots and the dough isn't sticky when you touch it, add more buttermilk.

Dust a surface with all-purpose flour and turn the dough out onto the surface. Flour your hands, then cuddle the dough by pressing your hands around the outer edges. Pat and press the top of the dough with your floured hands. Fold the dough in half, pat it, and fold it again. Repeat this two or three times until the outside of the dough feels less sticky and becomes smooth.

Use a rolling pin or pat the dough to flatten it ½ inch thick. Cut the biscuits using a 1-inch biscuit cutter without twisting the cutter. Place the biscuits in the cake pan or baking sheet so they touch if you like soft sides or about ½ inch apart for crisper sides.

Combine the leftover pieces of dough and cuddle them with your hands, handling the dough as little as possible. Cut more biscuits. Form the remaining scraps into a snake and place it around the biscuits. This will make the biscuits rise more evenly. (And the snake makes a crispy extra for the cook.)

Bake until lightly browned, 15–20 minutes.

Slice each biscuit in half horizontally once the biscuits have cooled slightly and spread with pimento cheese.

Chicken Pot Pie with
Cheddar Biscuit Topping

Forget piecrust topping—good flaky biscuits with cheddar cheese give flavor to pot pie. I like the doughy biscuit soaked in chicken broth. If you don't, bake the biscuits separately and spoon the filling over the biscuits shortcake-style.

MAKES 4–6 SERVINGS

FOR THE FILLING

1 tablespoon olive oil

1 small sweet onion, finely chopped

8 ounces button mushrooms, sliced

$1\frac{1}{2}$ cups water

$\frac{1}{2}$ ounce concentrated chicken stock or
demi-glace concentrate

1 sprig fresh thyme

1 sprig fresh tarragon, about $1\frac{1}{2}$ inches long

2 boneless, skinless cooked chicken thighs,
diced into $\frac{1}{2}$-inch pieces

2 medium carrots, sliced

2 tablespoons all-purpose flour

2 tablespoons cream

1 cup fresh or frozen and thawed peas

FOR THE BISCUIT TOPPING

1 cup soft wheat self-rising flour

$\frac{1}{2}$ cup shredded cheddar cheese

$\frac{1}{2}$ cup cream

All-purpose flour for dusting

Preheat the oven to 425°. Use a 2-quart baking dish.

Heat the olive oil in a Dutch oven over medium heat. Add the onions and cook until tender, about 5 minutes. Stir in the mushrooms and continue cooking for 8 minutes or until the liquid releases from the mushrooms. Add the water, chicken stock, thyme, and tarragon. Bring to a boil. Stir in the chicken and carrots and reduce the heat to a simmer. Cook for 10 minutes or until the carrots are tender. Remove the thyme and tarragon sprigs.

Combine the flour with the cream in a small bowl and mix until the flour is no longer lumpy. Stir into the filling, then add the peas. Simmer for 10 minutes, stirring occasionally.

If desired, cool and then refrigerate the filling for later use.

To make the biscuit topping, combine the flour and cheese in a mixing bowl. Stir in the cream. The dough will be dry.

Dust a surface with all-purpose flour and turn the dough out onto the surface. Flour your hands, then cuddle the dough by pressing your hands around the outer edges. Pat and press the top of the dough with your floured hands. Fold the dough in half, pat it, and fold it again. Repeat this two or three times until the outside of the dough feels less sticky and becomes smooth.

On a large piece of wax paper, roll out the dough to the size that will cover the top of the dish you'll be using.

Place the filling in the baking dish. Lift up the wax paper and, gently holding the edges of the dough, turn it over on top of the dish so the dough covers the filling, then peel off the wax paper. Tuck the edges of the dough under so it doesn't overlap the rim of the dish.

Place in the oven and bake for 25 minutes, or if the filling was refrigerated, bake for 35 minutes. When the biscuit topping is done and the filling is bubbly, remove from the oven. Let stand for 10 minutes before serving.

Mom's Chicken and Dumplings

If the weather forecast says it might snow in the South, there's a community-wide panic and people empty grocery store shelves of milk and bread. Instead, my mom runs to the kitchen and cooks up some chicken and dumplings.

Likewise, if you're starting to get a cold, she makes chicken and dumplings. Your winter and cold-season cure might be chicken soup, matzoh ball soup, tom yum soup, or wonton soup, but in the South, it's chicken and flat dumplings. They may not really cure a cold, but the joy of eating them on a cold winter day will make you feel better, even if the forecast is wrong once again and there's no snow.

MAKES 6 SERVINGS

1 (3-pound) whole chicken

Kosher salt

4 cups chicken broth

2$\frac{1}{4}$ cups soft wheat self-rising flour, divided

$\frac{1}{4}$ cup vegetable shortening, cut into $\frac{1}{2}$-inch chunks and chilled for 15 minutes

1$\frac{1}{4}$ cups milk or cream, divided, plus more if needed

All-purpose flour for dusting

$\frac{1}{4}$ teaspoon freshly ground black pepper, or to taste

Place the chicken in a Dutch oven and cover with water. Add a pinch or two of salt. Bring the water to a boil and reduce the heat to simmer. Cook for 1 hour or until the chicken is done. Remove the chicken, leaving 4 cups broth in the Dutch oven. Debone the chicken once it cools enough to handle.

To make the dumplings, measure 2 cups of the flour into a large mixing bowl. Add the cold chunks of shortening and toss them in the flour to coat. Using a pastry blender or your fingertips, break up the chunks until they're about the size of peas.

Make a well in the center and pour in ¾ cup of the milk or cream. Starting at the sides of the bowl, use a spatula or wooden spoon to toss the flour over the milk. Continue to work in the flour from the sides of the bowl, just until the dough comes together.

If the dough starts to pull away from the sides of the bowl and sticks to your fingers, you have the right amount of milk. If there are dry spots and the dough isn't sticky when you touch it, add more milk.

Dust a surface with all-purpose flour and turn the dough out onto the surface. Flour your hands, then cuddle the dough by pressing your hands around the outer edges. Pat and press the top of the dough with your floured hands. Fold the dough in half, pat it, and fold it again. Repeat this two or three times until the outside of the dough feels less sticky and becomes smooth.

Use a rolling pin or pat the dough to flatten it as thin as possible, about ⅛ inch thick.

Bring the broth to a boil. Cut the dough into 2- × 1-inch strips. Dip each strip in flour and drop it into the boiling broth.

Simmer for 20 minutes or until cooked through, stirring occasionally. Combine ¼ cup of the flour with ½ cup of the milk or cream until smooth. Add to the dumplings and cook until thickened. Stir in the chicken and pepper and heat until warm.

Lamb Stew with Caramelized Onion–Mashed Potato Dumplings

I once visited an amazing old restaurant in the small village of Hope, England. With its unmatched chairs, low ceiling, thick stone walls, and fire burning in the fireplace, it was the picture of Old World dining. Being in such a cozy pub called for ordering a stew with braised lamb and leeks, and it was as amazing as you would expect. Upon returning home, I made a simple stew and topped it with mashed potato dumplings seasoned with caramelized onions, a combination that reminds me of that visit.

MAKES 6 SERVINGS

FOR THE STEW

3 tablespoons olive oil

1 onion, chopped

1 leek, chopped

¼ cup all-purpose flour

1 teaspoon salt

¼ teaspoon freshly ground black pepper

1 pound lamb shoulder chops, cut into 1-inch pieces

2 cups water

½ ounce concentrated beef broth or demi-glace concentrate

12 ounces brown ale or Guinness

2 sprigs of thyme

1 potato, peeled and cut into 1-inch cubes

2 carrots, sliced into ½-inch slices

FOR THE DUMPLINGS

¾ cup soft wheat self-rising flour

¼ teaspoon freshly ground black pepper

¾ cup mashed potatoes

¼ cup buttermilk

¼ cup shredded Irish cheddar cheese

½ teaspoon minced fresh mint

To make the stew, place a Dutch oven over medium heat and add the olive oil. Cook the onions and leeks in the hot oil until caramelized and browned, about 30 minutes. Remove and reserve.

Place the flour, salt, and pepper in a shallow pan and toss the lamb in the flour. Add the lamb to the Dutch oven and cook until the meat is browned, about 5 minutes. Add the water, beef broth, beer, thyme, and half of the onion and leek mixture. Simmer for 1½ hours. Remove the thyme sprigs.

Add the potatoes and carrots and cook for about 20 minutes or until they're tender.

To make the dumplings, combine the flour and black pepper in a large mixing bowl. In another bowl, combine the mashed potatoes, buttermilk, cheese, and remaining half of the onion and leek mixture. Stir the buttermilk mixture into the flour. Drop by heaping tablespoons on top of the stew. Cover and cook for 20 minutes. Sprinkle the top with mint and serve.

Southern Beef Wellington

Fred Thompson, who has written about a dozen cookbooks, once went to the grocery store for buttermilk and returned shouting, "I have a great idea for dinner!" He had purchased duck pâté, steaks, mushrooms, and shallots for a deconstructed beef Wellington.

His southern twist on a classic made a beautiful presentation. The sauce is so good that I could think of a million excuses to make it. He has used it for years anytime he serves steak. The neighbors all talk about it and call it "The Sauce."

MAKES 4 OR 6 SERVINGS

FOR THE SAUCE

3 tablespoons olive oil, divided
8 ounces crimini mushrooms, sliced
1 tablespoon minced garlic (about 2 cloves)
1 tablespoon fresh thyme leaves
4 shallots, sliced into 1-inch strips
½ teaspoon sugar
2 tablespoons balsamic vinegar
2 tablespoons unsalted butter

FOR THE BISCUITS

Flaky Butter Biscuits (page 36)
5 ounces duck liver pâté

FOR THE STEAKS

4 or 6 steaks
Salt and freshly ground black pepper

To prepare the sauce, you'll need to cook the mushrooms and shallots separately at the same time in 2 large sauté pans. Add 1½ tablespoons olive oil to each pan.

Add the mushrooms and minced garlic to one pan and cook over medium heat, stirring occasionally, until the mushrooms lose their liquid and the liquid evaporates, about 20 minutes. Stir in the thyme and remove from the heat.

Add the shallots and the sugar to the other pan and cook over medium-low heat until the shallots are lightly caramelized and golden brown, about 20 minutes. Stir in the balsamic vinegar and remove from the heat.

Combine the mushrooms and shallots in one pan and stir in the butter.

Preheat the oven to 450°. Use a baking sheet with a silicone liner.

To prepare the biscuits, make the Flaky Butter Biscuits, but after the last fold, roll the dough into a rectangle ¼ inch thick and cut the dough in half. Slice the pâté into thin slices and place it in a single layer on half of the dough, then place the other half on top. Cut into 4 or 6 evenly sized squares, depending on the number of servings needed. Place on the baking sheet and bake for 20–25 minutes or until light brown.

To prepare the steaks, season with salt and pepper to taste. Grill or pan sear until medium rare.

To assemble, place each biscuit on a serving plate, lay a steak on top of the biscuit, and generously top with the sauce.

Heirloom Tomato Pie

Heirloom tomatoes have become the darlings of backyard garden-ers and farmers' markets because of their full tomato flavor. I like Cherokee Purple tomatoes because of their dark color, meaty tex-ture, and sweet flavor, not to mention their interesting history.

Cherokee Purple tomatoes came on the market in the early 2000s because John Green from Sevierville, Tennessee, mailed some seeds to Craig LeHoulier (a.k.a. The Tomato Man). Green said Cherokee Indians had given the seeds to their neighbors 100 years ago. Le-Houlier, who lives in Raleigh, North Carolina, is a seed saver who has thousands of varieties of tomato seeds. He offered the seeds to seed companies, and they came flooding onto the market.

For this tomato pie, use Cherokee Purple tomatoes or any flavor-ful heirloom variety.

MAKES 6 SERVINGS

1 cup all-purpose flour

1 teaspoon baking powder

$\frac{1}{2}$ teaspoon salt, plus more for the tomatoes

$\frac{1}{2}$ cup plus 3 tablespoons mayonnaise, divided

$\frac{1}{3}$ cup whole milk

3 large heirloom tomatoes

1 cup grated sharp cheddar cheese

1 tablespoon finely chopped fresh basil

Freshly ground black pepper

Preheat the oven to 350°. Use a 9-inch cast-iron skillet or baking dish.

Whisk together the flour, baking powder, and salt in a large mixing bowl. Add 3 tablespoons of the mayonnaise and the milk, stirring until the mixture just forms a dough. Gather the dough into a ball, and press it along the bottom and sides of the skillet or baking dish.

Peel the tomatoes by blanching them in boiling water for a few seconds until the skin can be easily removed, then slice them into ¼-inch slices. Remove the seeds, salt lightly, and drain on paper towels. Pat as dry as possible.

Combine the cheddar cheese, basil, and ½ cup of the mayonnaise in a small bowl.

Arrange half of the tomatoes on top of the dough in the skillet, overlapping, and sprinkle with salt and pepper. Top with half of the cheese mixture. Continue layering with the remaining tomatoes and cheese.

Bake until the cheese is melted and bubbly and the crust is brown, about 20–25 minutes.

Fried Green Tomato, Bacon, and Goat Cheese Biscuits

While you're waiting for your tomatoes to ripen, you can pick a few green ones for this dish. Southern chefs have been combining tangy goat cheese and tart fried green tomatoes for a while now, so I decided to try making a goat cheese biscuit filled with crunchy tomato and bacon, an early-season bacon and tomato sandwich.

MAKES 6 BISCUITS

FOR THE BISCUITS

2 cups all-purpose flour

1 tablespoon baking powder

½ teaspoon salt

2 ounces goat cheese, crumbled

½ cup whole milk, plus more if needed

½ cup cream

All-purpose flour for dusting

Melted butter for brushing the tops

FOR THE FRIED GREEN TOMATOES

1 large egg, lightly beaten

½ cup milk

½ cup all-purpose flour

½ cup cornmeal

1 teaspoon salt

½ teaspoon freshly ground black pepper

3 medium green tomatoes, sliced into ¼-inch slices

Bacon drippings or vegetable oil

Crumbled goat cheese

FOR THE SANDWICH

6 slices bacon, cooked until crisp

Preheat the oven to 500°. Use a nonstick cake pan or baking sheet.

To make the biscuits, whisk together the flour, baking powder, and salt in a large mixing bowl. Cut in the goat cheese until it's the size of peas.

Make a well in the center and pour in the milk and cream. Starting at the sides of the bowl, use a spatula or wooden spoon to toss the flour over the milk. Continue to work in the flour from the sides of the bowl, just until the dough comes together.

If the dough starts to pull away from the sides of the bowl and sticks to your fingers, you have the right amount of milk. If there are dry spots and the dough isn't sticky when you touch it, add more milk.

Dust a surface with all-purpose flour and turn the dough out onto the surface. Flour your hands, then cuddle the dough by pressing your hands around the outer edges. Pat and press the top of the dough with your floured hands. Fold the dough in half, pat it, and fold it again. Repeat this two or three times until the outside of the dough feels less sticky and becomes smooth.

Use a rolling pin or pat the dough to flatten it ½ inch thick. Cut the biscuits using a 3-inch biscuit cutter without twisting the cutter. Place the biscuits in the cake pan or baking sheet so they touch if you like soft sides or about ½ inch apart for crisper sides.

Combine the leftover pieces of dough and cuddle them with your hands, handling the dough as little as possible. Cut more biscuits. Form the remaining scraps into a snake and place it around the biscuits. This will make the biscuits rise more evenly. (And the snake makes a crispy extra for the cook.)

Bake the biscuits in the center of the oven until they're light golden brown, 8–10 minutes. Brush the tops with melted butter.

To make the fried green tomatoes, combine the egg and milk in a small bowl. Mix the flour, cornmeal, salt, and pepper in a shallow pan. Dredge the tomatoes in the flour mixture, dip them in the egg mixture, then dredge them in the flour mixture again.

Pour the bacon drippings or vegetable oil ⅛ inch deep in a large frying pan and heat to 350°. Drop the tomatoes in batches into the hot oil. When crispy and golden brown, remove and drain on paper towels. Sprinkle with additional goat cheese.

Assemble the biscuits by slicing each biscuit in half horizontally and placing 1 fried green tomato topped with goat cheese and 1 slice of bacon broken in half in the center of each biscuit.

Caramelized Onion, Bacon, and Biscuit Breakfast Casserole

Breakfast isn't just for breakfast anymore. Eggs and bacon have become all-day foods. It's fun to have breakfast for dinner. Of course, it's good in the morning too.

MAKES 6 SERVINGS

½ pound bacon
1 small onion, diced
½ red bell pepper, diced
1 clove garlic, minced
3 large eggs
½ cup whole milk
½ teaspoon sage
Salt and freshly ground black pepper to taste
3 cups baked biscuits, cut into 1½-inch chunks
½ cup shredded Guyère cheese

Preheat the oven to 350°. Coat an 8-inch square baking dish with nonstick cooking spray.

In a skillet over low heat, cook the bacon and remove to drain, reserving the drippings.

Add the onions to the skillet and cook over medium heat for about 20 minutes, until browned. Add the bell peppers and cook until tender. Add the garlic and cook for about 30 seconds.

Whisk the eggs, milk, sage, salt, and pepper in a deep bowl.

Crumble the biscuits into the prepared baking dish. Top with crumbled bacon, then the onion mixture, then the cheese. Pour the egg mixture over the top. Let stand for 15 minutes while the biscuits soak up the egg mixture. You may need to press the biscuits into the liquid with a spoon if they float.

Bake in the center of the oven for 30–35 minutes or until a knife inserted into the casserole comes out clean. Cool for 10 minutes and serve.

Sweet Biscuits and Desserts

In the land of sweet tea, brown sugar–rubbed pork, and cakes for every occasion, is it any surprise that sweet biscuits would be on the menu? As a lover of all things sweet, I like my biscuits dripping with honey or strawberry jam as the sweet ending to breakfast.

A collection of biscuit recipes would be incomplete without recipes for fried pies, cobblers, shortcakes, and bread puddings made from biscuits. The close cousin of a biscuit, the scone is also an obvious choice. If you've always eaten sponge cake as shortcake, try biscuits instead to soak up the sweet strawberry juice. If you've only had cobbler with piecrust, biscuits on top are much more interesting. I can never get enough of biscuits with fruit.

In this selection of biscuit desserts, I even manage to get chocolate into the mix.

Fried Pumpkin Pies

When I was growing up, every little market had some version of a fried pie, traditionally cooked in a cast-iron skillet. Daddy used to take us to his office at Calloway's Television Repair Shop, where they offered fried pies and peanuts along with soft drinks for customers who were waiting for repairs.

We would drop the peanuts into the soft drinks and have them along with fried pies, usually apple but sometimes chocolate or lemon. It was a rare treat!

The filling is traditionally made of dried fruit soaked in liquid and reconstituted, but I often use jam, peanut butter and jelly, lemon curd, or canned pumpkin, as in this recipe. This is a perfect use for leftover pumpkin that you've roasted for a pie.

MAKES ABOUT 8 PIES

FOR THE DOUGH

- 2 cups all purpose flour
- 2 teaspoons baking powder
- 1 teaspoon salt
- 1/3 cup vegetable shortening, cut into 1/2-inch chunks and chilled for 15 minutes
- 3/4 cup milk, plus more if needed
- All-purpose flour for dusting

FOR THE FILLING

- 2 cups puréed pumpkin
- 1/3 cup firmly packed brown sugar
- 1 teaspoon ground cinnamon
- 1/8 teaspoon ground nutmeg
- 1/8 teaspoon ground allspice

FOR THE PIES
Milk for sealing the pies
Vegetable oil
¼ cup sugar
1 tablespoon ground cinnamon

To make the dough, whisk together the flour, baking powder, and salt in a large mixing bowl. Add the cold chunks of shortening to the flour. Using a pastry blender or your fingertips, break up the chunks until they're about the size of peas.

Make a well in the center and pour in the milk. Starting at the sides of the bowl, use a spatula or wooden spoon to toss the flour over the milk. Continue to work in the flour from the sides of the bowl, just until the dough comes together.

If the dough starts to pull away from the sides of the bowl and sticks to your fingers, you have the right amount of milk. If there are dry spots and the dough isn't sticky when you touch it, add more milk.

Dust a surface with all-purpose flour and turn the dough out onto the surface. Flour your hands, then cuddle the dough by pressing your hands around the outer edges. Pat and press the top of the dough with your floured hands. Fold the dough in half, pat it, and fold it again. Repeat this two or three times until the outside of the dough feels less sticky and becomes smooth.

Use a rolling pin or pat the dough to flatten it ⅛ inch thick. Cut the dough using a 3-inch biscuit cutter without twisting the cutter.

To make the filling, combine the pumpkin, brown sugar, cinnamon, nutmeg, and allspice in a small bowl. Spoon a heaping tablespoon of the filling into the center of each piece of dough. Brush around the edges with milk. Fold the dough in half and press firmly. Use the tines of a very small fork to seal the edges and then turn. Seal the other side with the tines of the fork. Press lightly to distribute the filling throughout pocket.

In a large, heavy, deep-sided skillet over medium heat, add vegetable oil to a depth of ¼ inch. Heat to 365°. Gently add the pies 3 at a time to allow plenty of space between each. (The oil should come about halfway up the pies.) Cook for 3 minutes, turn, and cook for 3 more minutes or until both sides are golden brown. Remove from the pan and drain on a rack or paper towels.

Mix together the sugar and cinnamon in a small bowl and sprinkle over the tops. Allow the pies to cool for at least 10 minutes before eating.

Biscuit Shortcakes with Fresh Strawberries and Vanilla Cream

At some point every spring, berries are at that once-a-year perfect moment. Now a local farmer has started growing hothouse strawberries, so some darn good local berries are available in January. What was once just a springtime dessert has become a winter treat as well. In the winter, I serve the shortcakes warm; in the summer, I let them cool.

MAKES 4 LARGE SHORTCAKES

FOR THE BISCUITS

2 cups soft wheat self-rising flour

2 tablespoons sugar

8 tablespoons unsalted butter, cut into $1/2$-inch chunks and chilled for 15 minutes

$3/4$ cup heavy cream, plus 2 tablespoons for brushing the tops

All-purpose flour for dusting

Sugar for sprinkling on the tops

FOR THE FILLING

4 cups strawberries, stemmed, washed, and sliced

$2/3$ cup sugar

$2/3$ cup orange juice

1 teaspoon finely grated orange zest (optional)

FOR THE VANILLA CREAM

$1/2$ cup heavy cream

$1/3$ cup sugar

1 tablespoon pure vanilla extract

Pinch of salt

FOR THE SHORTCAKES

2 cups best-quality strawberry preserves

$2/3$ cup powdered sugar (optional)

Preheat the oven to 450°. Use a nonstick cake pan or baking sheet.

To make the biscuits, whisk together the flour and sugar in a large mixing bowl. Add the cold chunks of butter and toss them in the flour to coat. Using a pastry blender or your fingertips, break up the chunks until they're about the size of peas.

Make a well in the center and pour in the cream. Starting at the sides of the bowl, use a spatula or wooden spoon to toss the flour over the cream. Continue to work in the flour from the sides of the bowl, just until the dough comes together.

If the dough starts to pull away from the sides of the bowl and sticks to your fingers, you have the right amount of cream. The dough will seem slightly dry.

Dust a surface with all-purpose flour and turn the dough out onto the surface. Flour your hands, then cuddle the dough by pressing your hands around the outer edges. Pat and press the top of the dough with your floured hands. Fold the dough in half, pat it, and fold it again. Repeat this two or three times until the outside of the dough feels less sticky and becomes smooth.

Use a rolling pin or pat the dough to flatten it 1 inch thick.

Cut the biscuits using a 4-inch biscuit cutter without twisting the cutter. Place the biscuits in the cake pan or baking sheet so they touch if you like soft sides or about ½ inch apart for crisper sides. Cuddle the leftover pieces of dough with your hands, handling the dough as little as possible. Cut more biscuits. Brush the tops with cream and sprinkle with sugar.

Bake the biscuits in the center of the oven until they're light golden brown, 18–20 minutes. Move to a cooling rack to cool slightly.

To make the filling, in a medium bowl, toss the strawberries with the sugar, orange juice, and orange zest, if desired. Set aside.

To make the vanilla cream, combine all of the ingredients in the bowl of an electric mixer. Using the whisk attachment, whip the mixture until it forms soft peaks. Cover and refrigerate until ready to use.

To assemble the shortcakes, slice each biscuit in half horizontally. On the bottom half, add strawberry preserves, strawberry filling, and vanilla cream. Place the other half on top and top with additional strawberry filling and a spoonful of vanilla cream. If desired, dust the plate and biscuit with powdered sugar.

Cinnamon Rolls with Cream Cheese Frosting

Sweet dough rolled with butter, sugar, and cinnamon and frosted with sweet cream cheese that's socially acceptable for breakfast — who thought of that?

MAKES 9 CINNAMON ROLLS

FOR THE DOUGH

2 cups soft wheat self-rising flour

3 tablespoons sugar

6 tablespoons unsalted butter, cut into $\frac{1}{2}$-inch chunks and chilled for 15 minutes

$\frac{1}{2}$ cup whole milk, plus more if needed

All-purpose flour for dusting

FOR THE FILLING

3 tablespoons unsalted butter, at room temperature

$\frac{1}{3}$ cup sugar

1 tablespoon ground cinnamon

FOR THE FROSTING

1 tablespoon cream cheese, at room temperature

1 tablespoon whole milk

$\frac{3}{4}$ cup powdered sugar, sifted

Preheat the oven to 425°. Coat a 9-inch square baking pan with nonstick cooking spray.

To make the dough, whisk together the flour and sugar in a large mixing bowl. Add the cold chunks of butter to the flour and toss them to coat. Using a pastry blender or your fingertips, break up the chunks until they're about the size of peas.

Make a well in the center and add the milk. Starting at the sides of the bowl, use a spatula or wooden spoon to toss the flour over the milk. Continue to work in the flour from the sides of the bowl, just until the dough comes together.

If the dough starts to pull away from the sides of the bowl and sticks to your fingers, you have the right amount of milk. If there are dry spots and the dough isn't sticky when you touch it, add more milk.

Dust a surface with all-purpose flour and turn the dough out onto the surface. Flour your hands, then cuddle the dough by pressing your hands around the outer edges. Pat and press the top of the dough with your floured hands. Fold the dough in half, pat it, and fold it again. Repeat this two or three times until the outside of the dough feels less sticky and becomes smooth.

Roll the dough to a 10 × 14-inch rectangle.

To add the filling, spread the butter on top of the dough. Combine the sugar and cinnamon in a small bowl and sprinkle evenly over the butter. Starting at the 10-inch end, cut 9 even strips of dough, a little over 1 inch wide each. Roll each strip of dough into a snail and place each one cut-side down in the prepared baking pan, allowing about ½ inch between each roll.

Bake until light golden brown, about 12–14 minutes.

To make the frosting, in a medium bowl, stir together the cream cheese, milk, and powdered sugar until smooth. Spread over the hot rolls. Serve warm.

If you're not planning to eat all of the rolls immediately, cool the unfrosted rolls, wrap them tightly in plastic wrap, and store at room temperature; refrigerate the frosting. When you're ready to serve the rolls, heat them up, then frost them.

Peach Cobbler

Peaches are in the market for such a brief time that I end up buy-ing more than I can possibly eat so I have to make plenty of cob-bler. This is an old-fashioned recipe, just waiting for ice cream.

MAKES 6 SERVINGS

1 stick melted butter
1 cup all-purpose flour
2½ cups sugar, divided
2½ teaspoons baking powder
⅛ teaspoon salt
1 cup whole milk
2½ cups peeled, sliced peaches (about 6 peaches)

Preheat the oven to 350°. Coat a 2-quart baking dish with non-stick cooking spray.

Pour the melted butter into the prepared baking dish.

Whisk together the flour, 1¼ cups of the sugar, the baking powder, and the salt in a large mixing bowl. Add the milk and whisk until smooth.

Place the peaches in the prepared baking dish and spread the dough on top of the peaches. Sprinkle with the remaining 1¼ cups sugar. Bake for 25–30 minutes or until the top is lightly browned. Let stand for 10 minutes before serving. Top with ice cream if desired.

Spiced Fresh Peach–Pecan Biscuit Shortcakes

Shortcakes don't have to be limited to strawberries; peaches are good with them too. For this recipe, I spiced up the biscuits and added pecans for crunch.

MAKES 6 SERVINGS

FOR THE BISCUITS
2 cups soft wheat self-rising flour

¼ cup sugar

1 teaspoon ground cinnamon

⅛ teaspoon ground ginger

8 tablespoons unsalted butter, cut into ½-inch chunks and chilled for 15 minutes

½ cup chopped pecans

¾ cup buttermilk, plus more if needed

All-purpose flour for dusting

Melted butter for brushing the tops

FOR THE FILLING
6 small freestone peaches, peeled and sliced

¾ cup firmly packed brown sugar

½ teaspoon ground cinnamon

1 teaspoon lemon juice

FOR THE GINGER WHIPPED CREAM
1 cup heavy cream

¼ cup powdered sugar

¼ teaspoon ground ginger

1 teaspoon pure vanilla extract

Preheat the oven to 450°. Use a nonstick cake pan or baking sheet.

To make the biscuits, whisk together the flour, sugar, cinnamon, and ginger in a large mixing bowl. Add the cold chunks of butter and toss them in the flour to coat. Using a pastry blender or your fingertips, break up the chunks until they're about the size of peas. Stir in the pecans.

Make a well in the center and pour in the buttermilk. Starting at the sides of the bowl, use a spatula or wooden spoon to toss the flour over the buttermilk. Continue to work in the flour from the sides of the bowl, just until the dough comes together.

If the dough starts to pull away from the sides of the bowl and sticks to your fingers, you have the right amount of buttermilk. If there are dry spots and the dough isn't sticky when you touch it, add more buttermilk.

Dust a surface with all-purpose flour and turn the dough out onto the surface. Flour your hands, then cuddle the dough by pressing your hands around the outer edges. Pat and press the top of the dough with your floured hands. Fold the dough in half, pat it, and fold it again. Repeat this two or three times until the outside of the dough feels less sticky and becomes smooth.

Use a rolling pin or pat the dough to flatten it to the desired thickness: ½ inch for traditional biscuits or up to 1 inch for very tall biscuits.

Cut the biscuits using a biscuit cutter without twisting the cutter. Place the biscuits in the cake pan or baking sheet so they touch if you like soft sides or about ½ inch apart for crisper sides.

Combine the leftover pieces of dough and cuddle them with your hands, handling the dough as little as possible. Cut more biscuits. Form the remaining scraps into a snake and place it around the biscuits. This will make the biscuits rise more evenly. (And the snake makes a crispy extra for the cook.)

Bake the biscuits in the center of the oven until they're light golden brown, 12–14 minutes. Brush the tops with melted butter.

To make the filling, combine the peaches, sugar, cinnamon, and lemon juice in a medium bowl and let stand for at least 15 minutes.

To make the ginger whipped cream, combine the cream, sugar, ginger, and vanilla extract in a medium bowl and whip until stiff peaks form.

To assemble the shortcakes, slice each biscuit in half horizontally. On the bottom half, add the peach filling and ginger whipped cream, then place the other half on top.

Cream Scones

Coffee shops in the United States sell sweet triangle-shaped scones, but the origins of scones are in Scotland, where they're eaten with tea or as a dessert and can be sweet or savory. Close cousins of biscuits, scones are made using the same techniques. You can decide what you'd like to add to this basic recipe. If you can find it, clotted cream is still my favorite topping.

MAKES 6–8 SCONES

3 cups all-purpose flour

⅓ cup sugar, plus more for sprinkling on top

2 teaspoons baking powder

½ teaspoon salt

6 tablespoons unsalted butter, cut into ½-inch chunks and chilled for 15 minutes

¾ cup heavy cream, plus more for brushing the tops

1 large egg, lightly beaten

All-purpose flour for dusting

OPTIONAL ADD-INS

Finely chopped chocolate bar

Grated lemon zest and fresh blueberries

Grated orange zest and dried cranberries

Raisins and pecans

Scraped vanilla bean

Preheat the oven to 450°. Use a nonstick cake pan or baking sheet.

Whisk together the flour, sugar, baking powder, and salt in a large mixing bowl. Add the cold chunks of butter and toss them in the flour to coat. Using a pastry blender or your fingertips, break up the chunks until they're about the size of peas. If you're including additional ingredients, stir them in now.

Mix together the cream and egg in a small bowl. Make a well in the center of the flour mixture and pour in the cream and egg. Starting at the sides of the bowl, use a spatula or wooden spoon to toss the flour over the cream. Continue to work in the flour from the sides of the bowl, just until the dough comes together.

If the dough starts to pull away from the sides of the bowl and sticks to your fingers, you have the right amount of cream. The mixture will be slightly dry.

Dust a surface with all-purpose flour and turn the dough out onto the surface. Flour your hands, then cuddle the dough by pressing your hands around the outer edges. Pat and press the top of the dough with your floured hands. Fold the dough in half, pat it, and fold it again. Repeat this two or three times until the outside of the dough feels less sticky and becomes smooth.

Divide the dough in half. Use a rolling pin or pat each piece of dough to a round about 1 inch thick. Cut each round into 3–4 wedges. Place the wedges on the cake pan or baking sheet about ½ inch apart. Brush the tops with cream and sprinkle with sugar.

Bake the scones in the center of the oven until they're light golden brown, 12–14 minutes.

The Fat Elvis,
a.k.a. Taking Care of Biscuits

Biscuit lovers united to get their own event. The International Biscuit Festival began in 2010, when "Biscuit Boss" John Craig's longtime vision for a day honoring biscuits was brought to the streets of downtown Knoxville. John makes sure that biscuits take center stage. This isn't a fair—it's about the almighty biscuit.

At the festival, you can eat biscuits on Biscuit Boulevard made by local chefs. Try Loveless Café Biscuits, stop by for a Benton's ham biscuit made by Allan Benton himself, or get a ticket to a brunch hosted by the Inn at Blackberry Farm. The evening before the event, you can go to an elegant dinner at the inn with a six-course menu centered around biscuits, which ends with biscuit ice cream. The Food Network's Alton Brown even gave a biscuit talk at the 2012 gathering.

If that isn't enough, you can see some pretty amazing creations at the biscuit bake-off. Kimberly Pack won the first grand prize for this biscuit recipe. (I even have the Fat Elvis biscuit poster proudly displayed in my office.)

MAKES 10–12 SERVINGS

FOR THE BISCUITS

5$\frac{1}{3}$ tablespoons unsalted butter

2 cups soft wheat all-purpose flour

2 teaspoons baking powder

$\frac{1}{2}$ teaspoon baking soda

$\frac{1}{2}$ teaspoon salt

1$\frac{1}{2}$ cups powdered sugar

$\frac{1}{2}$ cup chopped honey-roasted peanuts

$\frac{1}{2}$ cup mashed bananas (about 1$\frac{1}{2}$ bananas)

$\frac{1}{2}$ cup buttermilk, plus more if needed

¼ cup powdered sugar

⅓ cup creamy peanut butter

1 tablespoon skim milk

¼ teaspoon pure vanilla extract

5–6 ripe bananas

10 slices bacon, cooked until crisp and cut in half

Put the butter in the freezer for about 30 minutes or longer before you start baking to give it time to get very cold and hard. If you have the space in your freezer, freeze the flour too.

Preheat the oven to 450°. Use a baking sheet with a silicone liner.

To make the biscuits, whisk together the flour, baking powder, baking soda, salt, and powdered sugar in a large mixing bowl. Grate the butter using a food processor with the grater attachment or a hand grater. Gently toss the butter into the flour using a wooden spoon. Stir in the peanuts.

Add the mashed bananas and buttermilk to a small bowl and stir just until blended. Add the mixture to the dough. If you need more buttermilk for the dough to pull together into a ball, add only a small amount and stir. The dough should come together but not be wet.

Pat the dough ½ inch thick. Cut the biscuits using a biscuit cutter without twisting the cutter and place them on the baking sheet about ½ inch apart so the sides brown.

Bake for 12–14 minutes, or until the tops are golden brown.

Meanwhile, to make the filling, combine the powdered sugar, peanut butter, milk, and vanilla extract in a small bowl.

To assemble the biscuits, cut each banana in half crosswise, then lengthwise. Slice each biscuit in half horizontally. On the bottom half, spread the filling and top with 2 banana slices and 2 bacon slices. Top with the other half.

Chocolate-Walnut Biscuit Bread Pudding

About 40 percent of food in the United States is thrown away, according to a 2012 report of the National Resource Defense Council. My grandmother would have a fit. She never threw away used aluminum foil, coffee cans, and such.

I've been baking so many biscuits that I needed to find uses for them. When I asked friends what they do with leftover biscuits, they often looked at me like I was crazy. It appears that having too many biscuits isn't a problem that most folks have. If you've made a batch or two of biscuits that came out dry, hard, ugly, or flawed in some way, here's what to do with them so you don't add to that 40 percent.

Sometimes I make this with half black walnuts and half regular walnuts. You can serve it warm or cold.

MAKES 12–16 SERVINGS

3 cups crumbled biscuits (about 6 biscuits)

1 cup milk

½ cup half-and-half

2 large eggs

½ cup sugar

½ cup firmly packed brown sugar

2 tablespoons unsweetened cocoa powder

1 teaspoon pure vanilla extract

¼ teaspoon kosher salt

½ cup chopped walnuts

1 cup semisweet chocolate chips

Preheat the oven to 350°. Coat a 9 × 5-inch loaf pan or two smaller loaf pans with nonstick cooking spray.

Crumble the biscuits into a deep bowl, and let them soak in the milk and half-and-half for 15 minutes. You may need to press the biscuits into the milk with a spoon if they float.

Whisk together the eggs, sugars, cocoa, vanilla extract, and salt in a small bowl, and stir into the milk and soft biscuits to make a batter. Let soak for 15 more minutes.

Stir in the nuts and chocolate chips just until combined. Pour into the prepared pan or pans.

For a 9 × 5-inch loaf pan, bake for 1 hour. For smaller pans, bake for 40–45 minutes, or until solid. If you insert a toothpick or knife to test for doneness, it should come out mostly clean, though the melted chocolate may coat it a bit.

Cool for about 15 minutes and serve topped with whipped cream.

Biscuit Toppers

If you really want to go to food heaven, top a biscuit with gravy or jam or sorghum or butter. So many things are good on biscuits that I could write a whole book on them. These are just a few of my favorites.

Grandma's Gravy

My mother, Tommie Ellis, makes gravy that doesn't have sausage or bacon in it; it's pure white with bits of pepper. This type of milk or white gravy is often used for biscuits, but it's also served with chicken and other meat dishes. My daughter calls it Grandma's Gravy, in part to separate it from everyday fare and elevate it to a special-occasion dish that we would have only at her grandmother's house.

In culinary terms, the base of the gravy is a roux made from pork fat and flour. Essentially, it's a béchamel sauce, a classic used in cuisines throughout the world. But in southern cooking, it's just the stuff of Grandma's cookin'.

MAKES 4 HEARTY SERVINGS

---

8 slices bacon

4 sausage patties

$1/3$ cup rendered bacon and sausage fat

$1/3$ cup all-purpose flour

$3\frac{1}{2}$ cups milk

Kosher salt and freshly ground black pepper

Cook the bacon and sausage over medium heat in a large, heavy skillet. Remove and drain on paper towels, reserving the rendered fat. Return $1/3$ cup of the fat to the skillet. Add the flour and stir constantly until it smells slightly nutty but isn't browned, about 4 minutes.

Very gradually pour in the milk while stirring. Stir constantly until the gravy begins to thicken, about 10 minutes. Add salt and pepper to taste.

Split a biscuit and spoon the gravy over the top. Serve the bacon and sausage on the side.

Sawmill Gravy

According to folklore, sawmill gravy traces its roots to Appalachian logging camps where a little bit of sausage had to feed a hungry crew of workmen. In the poor communities of the South, biscuits and gravy were a way to use a little meat to feed a lot of people. Now most of us work in offices, but we still love a plate of biscuits and gravy every now and then.

I got this recipe from chef Kyle Wilkerson, who learned to make it from his grandmother. He says she still makes it just about every week.

MAKES 4 SERVINGS

1 pound bulk breakfast sausage
2 tablespoons rendered sausage fat
2 tablespoons all-purpose flour
2 cups whole milk
Kosher salt and freshly ground black pepper

Cook the sausage in a large, heavy skillet over medium-low heat, crumbling it as you cook. Cook until very crisp, almost dry, about 30 minutes. Remove the sausage to drain on paper towels, reserving the rendered fat. Return 2 tablespoons of the fat to the skillet. Stir in the flour and cook until it smells nutty, about 4 minutes. Gradually add the milk while whisking vigorously and continue to whisk until thickened. Add salt and pepper to taste.

Split a biscuit and spoon the gravy over the top.

Tomato Gravy

While tomato gravy is tomato sauce in Italian culture, in the South, it's a roux-based gravy with bacon fat, flour, and tomatoes. I like to add other flavors and a bit of milk. I've made a vegan version using canola oil instead of bacon fat and milk. This gravy is good over biscuits or cornbread.

MAKES 4 SERVINGS

2 tablespoons rendered bacon fat

1 small onion, finely chopped

2 cloves garlic, finely chopped

1 teaspoon kosher salt

½ teaspoon freshly ground black pepper

1 teaspoon finely chopped fresh thyme

1 teaspoon finely chopped fresh basil

2 tablespoons all-purpose flour

3 cups seeded, chopped tomatoes

½ cup milk

Place the bacon fat in a large, heavy skillet over medium heat. Add the onions and cook until tender. Add the garlic, salt, pepper, thyme, and basil and cook for 1 minute. Stir in the flour and cook for 4 minutes. Stir in the tomatoes and cook until they soften, about 5 minutes.

Gradually add the milk. Season with additional salt and pepper if desired.

Split a biscuit and spoon the gravy over the top.

Sorghum Butter

Sorghum is a star that needs to make a comeback. Contrary to popular belief, sorghum is not the same thing as molasses, which is a by-product of the sugar industry. Sorghum is a grass, and sweet sorghum cane syrup is the traditional biscuit sweetener in the South. It's packed with nutrients—1 tablespoon contains 30 mg of calcium, as well as iron, zinc, and magnesium.

Yet it has fallen out of mainstream eating. A century ago, the United States produced 10 million gallons of sorghum a year, but now less than a million gallons are produced each year. At Muddy Pond Sorghum Mill in Tennessee, Mark and Sherry Guenther grow the cane, operate the mill, and spread the word about the health benefits of their syrup. They do demonstrations using horses for milling, but they have a modern milling operation as well. He says he eats sorghum on everything, except he doesn't put it in his coffee.

It's good alone on biscuits, so I decided to make sorghum butter. I spread it on biscuits or, like Mark Guenther, just about anything.

MAKES ABOUT 1 CUP

1 stick salted butter, at room temperature
4 tablespoons sorghum syrup

Whip the butter using an electric mixer until it's light and soft. Reduce the speed and drizzle in the sorghum. Put the butter into a container and refrigerate. Keep airtight, and it will keep as long as regular butter.

Strawberry Freezer Jam

This jam is frozen, so no canning is necessary. It's simple to make and one of the best biscuit toppers ever. We run out of it every year about midwinter and vow to make more the following year. No matter how much of it we make, though, we still seem to run out.

MAKES 4 PINTS

2 cups crushed strawberries

4 cups sugar

2 tablespoons lemon juice

1 (1.75-ounce) package fruit pectin

¾ cup water

Stir together the strawberries, sugar, and lemon juice in a large mixing bowl.

Combine the pectin and water in a medium saucepan and bring to a boil, stirring constantly. Boil for 1 minute, then pour over the fruit and stir well.

Spoon the jam into freezer-safe jars, leaving about ½-inch space at the top. Screw the lids on tightly and refrigerate for 24 hours, then place in the freezer. The jam can be frozen for up to a year.

Acknowledgments

This book has been a lifetime in the making, so it's with heartfelt appreciation that I thank the people in my life who taught me how to make biscuits and the importance of sharing food, especially my mom, Tommie Ellis.

I want to thank my daughter, Katrina Moore, for her edits and encouragement and for growing up sampling my experiments and telling people her mom makes great biscuits without adding, "mostly at work."

I've had the chance to learn from so many people who shared their recipes, including Sharon Benton, Shirley Corriher, Colleen Cruze, John Egerton, Tommie Ellis, Nina Swan-Kohler, Kyle Wilkerson, and Lynn Winter. Thanks also to John Craig, the "Biscuit Boss."

I especially owe appreciation to Elaine Maisner, my editor, who guided me every step of the way, and to Kim Bryant, who designs and inspires. I also owe a debt of gratitude to Nathalie Dupree, who has always told me I could write a biscuit book.

I wouldn't be where I am today without the support of Fred Thompson, who has encouraged me while I chased my dream of writing. He has read drafts of the book more than once and offered suggestions, until he finally said, "It's good. Stop working on it."

Index